Joseph Smith

Impressions of a Prophet

Joseph Smith

Impressions of a Prophet

Art and commentary by Liz Lemon Swindle
Text by Susan Easton Black

Deseret Book Company
Salt Lake City, Utah

Library of Congress Cataloging-in-Publication Data

Swindle, Liz Lemon, 1953–

    Joseph Smith : Impressions of a prophet / art and commentary by Liz Lemon

Swindle ; text by Susan Easton Black.

      p.   cm.

    Includes bibliographical references.

    ISBN 1-57345-316-1

    1. Smith, Joseph, 1805–1844. 2. Mormons—United States—

Biography. I. Black, Susan Easton. II. Title.

BX8695.S6L46   1998   97-46357

                                                    CIP

42316

Printed in the United States of America

10 9 8 7 6 5 4 3 2 1

Table of Contents

Introduction   1

1 ☙ The Boy   4

2 ☙ A Visionary Youth   12

3 ☙ The Book of Mormon   22

4 ☙ The Church   34

5 ☙ The Gathering   40

6 ☙ Glory and Tribulation   56

7 ☙ In Prison   68

8 ☙ Nauvoo   80

9 ☙ The Martyrdom   92

Bibliography   106

Acknowledgments

M Y DEEPEST GRATITUDE goes out to my husband, Jon. Artists can be tough to live with. His patience, love, and support have kept me going when I wanted to quit. He believed in me when this art was just a dream. Without him, this project would still be little more than a dream. Thank you. 🖊 My thanks to Repartee Galleries and Foundation Arts for their help in making the project come together. A special thanks to John and Sharon Swindle, whose help and patience were the glue that held the project together. Their often-unrecognized long hours and untiring efforts have touched me deeply. 🖊 My thanks to Kenneth Cope for his inspiring music that first touched my soul and made me wonder who Joseph Smith really was, and to Susan Easton Black for saying in words what my heart longs to say. To both of you, thank you for your friendship and support. Knowing you has made my life better. 🖊 Janita Anderson kept late nights and long hours to bring the project to public attention. She is an incredible publicist and a dear friend. Jim Sherman is my photographer and good friend. His ideas and vision have made the difference in the way the paintings look today. His willingness to help where others would not is a testament to his goodness and love. 🖊 My thanks to my models Cliff Cole and Jennifer Hohl, whose portrayals of Joseph and Emma have been filled with character and compassion. Their insights and feelings have brought to life the emotions you see in the paintings. To Cliff for his loyalty and friendship and to Jennifer for being my kindred spirit, thank you both. My thanks to Richard Wilson, who portrayed Hyrum Smith, and to all my models and stand-ins, who endured hot and cold weather in funny-looking costumes. 🖊 To Emma, I thank you for your undying devotion to your husband, the Prophet Joseph, and your quiet strength. To Joseph, my friend, thank you. Finally, to my Heavenly Father, my gratitude for sticking by me when the going looked hopeless, and for the patience to teach me when I didn't want to be taught. Thank you for the strength to keep going and the determination to run faster than I thought I could. Thank you.

—LIZ LEMON SWINDLE

THE MAKING OF
JOSEPH SMITH: IMPRESSIONS OF A PROPHET

*I am continually amazed at how willingly we pass by life's rare moments of
inspiration as we struggle to make it through another day. In my life
I have found that my greatest moments of spiritual growth come when I have
hit the spiritual wall. It seems that hitting this wall is the way the
Lord has of stopping me long enough to realize what I have been missing.*
*In early August 1994 I had hit the wall in a way that stopped me in
my tracks. It was at this moment that I listened to a song entitled "Brothers"
by Kenneth Cope.*   *Now, when I say* listen, *I should clarify. I had
heard the song many times, but on this afternoon I truly heard the message of
the song for the first time. "Brothers" tells of the relationship between
the Prophet Joseph Smith and his brother Hyrum.*   *I began thinking of
my own sons and the love they have for each other. Joseph and Hyrum
somehow seemed real to me in a way I had never felt before. Looking back on
my life as a member of the Church, I realized that I had shown very
little interest in Joseph or in the history of the Church he restored. I was unknowingly turning away from the quiet glimpses of eternity, always on my
way to somewhere else.*   *I don't know exactly when this project went from
one painting to more than thirty paintings of the life of Joseph Smith.
And I am not sure when my testimony of the Prophet Joseph Smith turned from
a single moment of curiosity into a multitude of powerful witnesses.
All the same, I know that Joseph Smith is indeed the Lord's prophet called to
restore this gospel to the earth. Through his sufferings and the sufferings
of his family, we each benefit eternally. I am grateful to the Prophet and grateful
to our Lord, who made Joseph's mission and work a reality.*

—LIZ LEMON SWINDLE

**ay 16, 1995, Hiram, Ohio.** The camera rolls, and actors portraying Joseph Smith and a lawless mob reenact the tarring and feathering of the Mormon prophet in the rural community. As Joseph cries, "You will have mercy and spare my life," the other men laugh, and one calls out, "Call on yer God for help; we'll show ye no mercy." Tar is poured over his body. The moment is recorded on film, and the actors rise to their feet.

The scene is one of many captured by film crews and professional directors who assist Utah artist Liz Lemon Swindle in conveying with paint and brush the images in her gallery display *Joseph Smith: Impressions of a Prophet.* By studying photographic prints of historic reenactments, Liz creates in her portraits an unusually authentic representation of events in the life of the Prophet of the Restoration. Liz has been on site with actors, cameras, and documentation to film reenactments of major events of Joseph Smith's life, from his early beginnings in Vermont to his death in Carthage.

Most memorable to the Utah artist have been the many on-site scenes that call for children to play major roles. Engaging in activities such as snowball fights, pulling sticks, fishing, and playing ball, Joseph often interrupted what Jesse W. Crosby, an acquaintance of the Prophet, called his "important work" to spend time with children and help around the home. "Some of the home habits of the Prophet—building kitchen fires, carrying

out ashes, carrying in wood and water, assisting in the care of the children," wrote Crosby in disgust, "were not in accord with my idea of a great man's self-respect."[1]

Children disagreed with Crosby, and so did thousands of early members of The Church of Jesus Christ of Latter-day Saints. They felt blessed that they "could see the face of a Prophet, such as had lived on the earth in former times, a man that had revelations, to whom the heavens were opened, who knew God and His character," and who also nurtured children and was not above household chores.[2] For them, his human kindness or jovial nature did not detract from his dignity as a prophet of God. One early member, Emmeline B. Wells, recalled meeting Joseph: "The one thought that filled my soul was, I have seen the Prophet of God, he has taken me by the hand, and this testimony has never left me in all the 'perils by the way.'"[3] Brigham Young, a close contemporary of the Mormon prophet, stated, "I feel like shouting hallelujah, all the time, when I think that I ever knew Joseph

Let's Get Papa

Smith, the Prophet whom the Lord raised up . . . , and to whom He gave keys and power to build up the kingdom of God on earth and sustain it."[4]

For Liz Lemon Swindle, visualizing the Prophet as he cared for a sick child or interrupted the translation of holy writ to play with children captures her attention and her heart. "I cannot imagine a better role model for children than the Prophet Joseph Smith," she says.

Liz, a well known and respected wildlife artist, has become the premier painter of Joseph Smith. The change of direction in her art was inspired by Utah composer and lyricist Kenneth Cope. As Liz listened to the lyrics of Cope's musical presentation *My Servant Joseph,* she became "intrigued with the view of Joseph Smith we rarely hear about—the family man." Listening to one song from the presentation, "Brothers," evoked in her an intense personal response, and her thoughts led her to set aside her wildlife paintings and illustrations and immerse herself in creating artistic vignettes of the Mormon prophet.

With cameras, actors, and paints, she has painted lifelike works of art. Her more than thirty portraits of the Mormon leader are the hallmarks of her creativity. "I know that Joseph Smith was the Lord's prophet called to restore His gospel to the earth. I am grateful for the life he lived and for the talent given me to portray that life with paint and canvas."

Sponsored by the Foundation Arts and Repartee Galleries, Liz's *Joseph Smith: Impressions of a Prophet* premiered in April 1997 at the Joseph Smith Memorial Building in Salt Lake City. The gallery display was next exhibited in the Independence Missouri Visitors Center and the Nauvoo Visitors Center before being shown at the Washington Temple Visitors Center. This book combines the paintings and drawings of Liz Lemon Swindle with Brigham Young University historian Susan Easton

 like to think Joseph Smith's children knew him as a father who not only loved them but shared his life with them. The Prophet of the Restoration was not too busy to be a family man. His children were never strangers to him. Like most devoted fathers, he enjoyed happy hours in his home.

Black's descriptions of the historical events related to each of the artworks. Liz's comments on the paintings also are included in sidebars throughout the book (similar to the one on this page). Dr. Black expresses her appreciation to the artist for the invitation to join her in a unique portrayal of the life of Joseph Smith.

Notes

1. Hyrum L. Andrus and Helen Mae Andrus, comps., *They Knew the Prophet* (Salt Lake City: Bookcraft, 1974), p. 145.

2. Brigham Young, in *Journal of Discourses,* 26 vols. (Liverpool: S. W. Richards, 1857), 4:104. Hereafter cited as *JD.*

3. *Young Woman's Journal* 16 (December 1905): 555.

4. Brigham Young, in *JD* 3:51.

CHAPTER ONE

J

OSEPH Smith, Jr., was

born December 23, 1805, in the rural setting of Sharon,

Windsor County, Vermont. Doctor Joseph A. Denison, a country

practitioner, reportedly assisted in the delivery. Years later he wrote in

his account book, "If I had known how he was going to turn out I'd have

smothered the little cuss."[1] The assisting doctor never understood that "it was

decreed in the councils of of eternity, long before the foundations of the earth were laid, that [Joseph Smith] should be the man, in the last dispensation of this world, to bring forth the word of God to the people, . . . [that] he was foreordained in eternity to preside over this last dispensation."[2]

From the writings of Lucy Mack Smith, it appears that she did not anticipate the prophetic calling of her newborn infant. "In the meantime we had a son," Lucy recorded, "whom we called Joseph after the name of his father."[3]

During the early years of Joseph's life, he lived with his family in a log cabin on a sloping prominence known as "Dairy Hill" in Sharon, Vermont. His father, Joseph Smith, Sr., supported the family by cultivating and improving a rented farm in the summer and by teaching school in the winter months. "In this way . . . our circumstances gradually improved," wrote Mother Smith, "until we found ourselves quite comfortable."[4]

ITH CONFIDENCE the family ventured from Sharon to other small towns in Vermont, hoping to improve their financial circumstances. In 1811 they moved twenty miles from Sharon to West Lebanon, New Hampshire, and for a brief season contemplated, "with joy and satisfaction, the prosperity which had attended our recent exertions; and we doubled our diligence, in order to obtain more of this world's goods."[5] Unfortunately, the hope of prosperity did not materialize, for "this state of things did not long continue."[6] A typhus fever epidemic that left nearly six thousand dead in its wake in the Connecticut Valley region

raged through the small community of Lebanon, afflicting children in the Smith household. Although the other children recovered from the illness without undue complications, young Joseph, who had the fever for two weeks, suffered from side effects much longer. A local doctor diagnosed one side effect as a sprained shoulder. His liniment remedy failed to relieve the problem, and soon a swelling appeared under Joseph's arm. Lancing the infected portion of his arm only added to the child's pain. "Oh, father! the pain is so severe," cried Joseph. "How can I bear it!"[7] Bear it he did, however, for "the disease removed and descended into my left leg and ancle and terminated in a fever sore of the worst kind."[8] Anxious about the discomfort of his brother, "Hyrum sat beside him [both] day and night . . . , holding the affected part of his leg in his hands and pressing it between them, so that [Joseph] might be enabled to endure the pain."[9]

Medical practitioners with varying degrees of expertise proposed amputation of his foot. Mother Smith refused to accept their proposal. The suggestion "was like a thunderbolt to me," she said.[10] Joseph also protested: "Young as I was, I utterly refused to give my assent to the operation." However, he "consented to [the doctors] Trying an experiment by removing a large portion of the bone from my left leg."[11] When his father learned of Joseph's consent to surgery, he turned "his eyes upon his boy, . . . burst into a flood of tears, and sobbed like a child."[12]

Secure in the knowledge of his father's love, Joseph refused to be tied to the bedstead during the operation. He insisted, "No, doctor, I will not be bound, for I can bear the operation much better if I have my liberty. . . . But I

CHILD OF PROMISE

As a mother, I've often wondered what Lucy's thoughts and feelings

were as she cradled Joseph in her arms. I have gazed upon my

own children and wondered what promises they might have made to their Heavenly

Father before leaving him, how they were prepared for their earthly missions,

and what I need to do to help them find their way back to Him.

Did Mother Smith, looking upon this precious child, know in

some small way the mission that was

before him? When we look upon

our own children, fresh from our

Heavenly Father, do we consider

how important our role as

a parent is?

will tell you what I will do—I will have my father sit on the bed and hold me in his arms, and then I will do whatever is necessary in order to have the bone taken out."[13]

The surgeons operated "by boring into the bone of his leg, first on one side of the bone where it was affected, then on the other side, after which they broke it off with a pair of forceps or pincers. They thus took away large

The turbulent epidemic in Lebanon that marred Joseph's childhood also reduced Father Smith to poverty and debt once again. "We were compelled to strain every energy to provide for our present necessities, instead of making arrangements for the future," recalled Lucy.[17]

Seeking economic freedom, the Smiths moved from Lebanon to Norwich, Windsor County, Vermont. In

Through young Joseph's prolonged illness, Father Smith was solicitous of his son's needs. Hours of caring must have led Joseph to choose his father's loving arms over the surgeon's medical advice. I believe it is from the example of Joseph Smith, Sr., that his son learned how to be a good father.

pieces of the bone."[14] During the surgery Mother Smith entered the room. "Oh, my God! what a spectacle for a mother's eye!" she wrote. "The wound torn open, the blood still gushing from it, and the bed literally covered with blood. Joseph was pale as a corpse."[15]

His recovery was slow and painful. "Fourteen additional pieces of bone afterwards worked out before my leg healed, during which time I was reduced so very low that my mother could carry me with ease."[16] Hoping that the sea breezes off the coast of Massachusetts would speed his recovery, Joseph was sent to live with his uncle Jesse Smith. After a brief season with Uncle Jesse, he showed signs of renewed strength and left Massachusetts to join his family. However, until his wounds healed, bed and crutches were his lot.

Norwich, the family worked on a rented farm, but this time without credit to tide them over until the first harvest. Adding to their difficulties, "the first year our crops failed; yet, by selling fruit which grew on the place, we succeeded in obtaining bread for the family. . . . The crops the second year were as the year before—a perfect failure. Mr. Smith now determined to plant once more, and if he should meet with no better success than he had the two preceding years, he would then go to the state of New York, where wheat was raised in abundance. The next year an untimely frost destroyed the crops . . . [and] almost caused a famine. This was enough," wrote Lucy. "My husband was now altogether decided upon going to New York."[18]

In 1816 Joseph Smith, Sr., left the Connecticut River Valley and settled in Palmyra, Ontario County, New York.[19]

My Father Will Hold Me

His family remained in Norwich for a short time until Caleb Howard, the man hired to convey Mother Smith and her eight children three hundred miles to Palmyra, was ready to begin the journey. On the journey Howard proved to be "an unprincipled and unfeeling wretch, by the way in which he handled both our goods and money, as well as by his treatment of my children, especially Joseph," wrote Lucy. "He would compel him to travel miles at a time on foot, notwithstanding he was still lame."[20]

Joseph vividly wrote of the cruelty he endured: "After [Howard] had got started on the journey with my mother & family, spent the money he had received of my father in drinking & gambling &c.— . . . [He] drove me from the wagon & made me travel in my weak state through the snow, 40 miles per day for several days, during which time I suffered the most excruciating weariness & pain, . . . when my brothers remonstrated with Mr. Howard, for his treatment to me, he would knock them down with the butt of his whip." Adding to Joseph's difficulties was the driver of a passing sleigh, who deliberately knocked him to the ground. "[I was] left to wallow in my blood," wrote Joseph. It was not "until a stranger came along" that the young boy was rescued. "[The stranger] picked me up, & carried me to the Town of Palmyra."[21]

In Palmyra Joseph, Sr., joined his family, who had arrived in the village with only "a small portion of our affects, and barely two cents in cash."[22] The Smiths were "much reduced—not from indolence, but on account of many reverses of fortune, with which our lives had been rather singularly marked. Notwithstanding our misfortunes, and the embarrassments with which we were surrounded," Mother Smith recalled, "I was quite happy once more having the society of my husband."[23]

With renewed courage the Smiths redoubled their efforts to gain financial stability. They wanted to be property owners, a dream that had eluded them since 1803. Father Smith opened a small shop on Main Street and sold gingerbread, pies, boiled eggs, and root beer to paying customers. Mother Smith painted and sold to admiring neighbors oilcloth coverings for tables and stands. Their sons worked as common laborers doing gardening and harvesting, rocking up wells, and taking on any odd jobs that paid cash. They also made and sold split-wood chairs, brooms, and baskets.

JOSEPH RECALLED those days of excessive toil: "Being in indigent circumstances [we] were obliged to labour hard for the support of [our] large Family . . . [and] it required the exertions of all [family members] that were able to render any assistance."[24] For a year and a half the family worked and saved for a down payment on a hundred-acre farm. The quality of their labors is best described by the recollections of Joseph's brother William Smith: "Whenever the neighbors wanted a good day's work done they knew where they could get a good hand."[25]

It was not long before Father Smith was able to begin making payments on some farm acreage he hoped to own one day. With easy terms on property valued between $700 and $900, the Smiths were confident good fortune had smiled upon them. The contract clause stating that "failure to meet the payment [gives] the land agent the legal right to reclaim the farm, improvements and all, with no compensation for the family's labor," seemed less than a remote possibility.[26]

The Smith farm was nestled in a wooded tract on Stafford Road less than two miles south of the village of Palmyra. Within the first year of residency, "we made nearly all of the first payment, erected a log house, and commenced clearing. I believe something like thirty acres of land were got ready for cultivation the first year," said Lucy. She added that by the second year "we had a snug loghouse, neatly furnished, and the means of living comfortably."[27] Thus, the Smiths, with "the strictest kind of economy and labor," turned the heavily wooded acreage into a productive farm "admired for its good order and industry."[28]

With productivity and apparent permanency in the community came a sense of belonging and neighborly cordiality. "The hand of friendship was extended on every side," wrote Lucy.[29] "If we might judge by external manifestations, we had every reason to believe that we had many good and affectionate friends for never have I seen more kindness or attention shown to any person or family than we received from those around us" in Palmyra.[30]

Notes

1. Quoted from a statement by John D. Spring, M.D., Nashau, New Hampshire, May 27, 1970, as cited in Larry C. Porter, "A Study of the Origins of The Church of Jesus Christ of Latter-day Saints in the States of New York and Pennsylvania, 1816–1831," Ph.D. diss., Brigham Young University, 1971, p. 19, 23n. Hereafter cited as Porter, New York Dissertation.

2. Brigham Young, in JD 7:289–90.

3. Lucy Mack Smith, History of Joseph Smith by His Mother, ed. Preston Nibley (Salt Lake City: Bookcraft, 1956), p. 46. Hereafter cited as Smith, History of Joseph Smith.

4. Ibid., p. 46.

5. Ibid., p. 51.

6. Ibid.

7. Ibid., p. 55.

8. Joseph Smith, "Manuscript History of the Church," Book A-1, p. 131; as quoted in Reed C. Durham Jr., "Joseph Smith's Own Story of a Serious Childhood Illness," BYU Studies 10 (Summer 1970): 481. Hereafter cited as Durham, "Joseph Smith's Own Story."

9. Smith, History of Joseph Smith, p. 55.

10. Ibid., p. 56.

11. Durham, "Joseph Smith's Own Story," p. 481.

12. Lucy Mack Smith, "Preliminary Manuscript of Biographical Sketches of Joseph Smith," typescript, p. 31, Archives Division, Church Historical Department, The Church of Jesus Christ of Latter-day Saints, Salt Lake City, Utah. Hereafter cited as Smith, "Preliminary Manuscript."

13. Smith, History of Joseph Smith, p. 57.

14. Ibid.

15. Ibid., p. 58.

16. Durham, "Joseph Smith's Own Story," p. 58.

17. Smith, History of Joseph Smith, p. 59.

18. Ibid.

19. See LaMar E. Garrard, "The Asael Smith Family Moves from Vermont to New York, 1806 to 1820," in Regional Studies in Latter-day Saint Church History: New York, ed. Larry C. Porter, Milton V. Backman, Jr., Susan Easton Black (Provo, Utah: Department of Church History and Doctrine, Brigham Young University, 1992), pp. 15–31.

20. Smith, History of Joseph Smith, p. 62.

21. Durham, "Joseph Smith's Own Story," p. 481.

22. Smith, History of Joseph Smith, p. 63.

23. Ibid.

24. Dean C. Jessee, comp., The Personal Writings of Joseph Smith (Salt Lake City: Deseret Book Co., 1984), p. 4.

25. J. W. Peterson, "William Smith Interview," Deseret Evening News, 20 January 1894, 28:11.

26. Lucy Mack Smith, Biographical Sketches of Joseph Smith, the Prophet, and His Progenitors for Many Generations (London and Liverpool: S. W. Richards, 1853 [reprint ed., New York: Arno Press and the New York Times, 1969]), pp. 70–71. Hereafter cited as Smith, Biographical Sketches.

27. Ibid., pp. 72–73.

28. Lucy Mack Smith, "Manuscript History of Her Son Joseph Smith, Jr.," as quoted by Donald L. Enders, "The Joseph Smith, Sr., Family: Farmers of the Genesee," Joseph Smith: The Prophet, The Man, ed. Susan Easton Black and Charles D. Tate, Jr. (Provo, Utah: Brigham Young University Religious Studies Center, 1993), p. 213.

29. Smith, History of Joseph Smith, p. 65.

30. Smith, "Preliminary Manuscript," p. 38.

CHAPTER TWO

TH E cordiality extended to the Smith family by neighbors and newfound friends ended abruptly in 1820. The dramatic change from friendly greetings to open confrontations began when fourteen-year-old Joseph announced to an itinerant minister that he had seen a heavenly vision. The minister treated his announcement lightly, as if it was a figment of the boy's imagination.[1] Grown men scoffed at the idea of heavenly beings appearing in the Palmyra woods. The unwavering affirmation of the teenager soon brought out the rancor of minister and farmer alike. Although these acquaintances of the Smiths espoused religious leanings and even claimed heavenly raptures, they were disturbed by the nature of the boy's vision. Perhaps they could have accepted a report from young Joseph of divine assurance of forgiveness and a promise of grace, but not a grand vision of God the Father and his Son Jesus Christ. Such a claim was beyond reason for professed Christians.

By 1820 the spirit of revivalism permeated even the most stoic sects in Palmyra. Men of the cloth preached of salvation, justice, and grace—not restoration. They spoke with a fervor that stirred the soul. Their chorus of believers shouted with conviction, "Hallelujah, brother, I've been saved." To one observer, Palmyra was a battleground for men's souls. "Lo, here! Lo, there!" was the sectarian cry.[2]

The revivalism in Palmyra "commenced with the Methodists, but soon became general among all the sects," wrote Joseph. "The whole district of country seemed affected by it, and great multitudes united themselves to the different religious parties, which created no small stir and division amongst the people."[3] Lucy Smith and her children Hyrum, Sophronia, and Samuel joined the popular Presbyterian church. Joseph "wanted to get Religion too, wanted to feel and shout like the rest but could feel nothing."[4]

"Priest contending against priest, and convert against convert" over conflicting Christian doctrine left him confused as to which denomination was accepted by God. "It was impossible for a person young as I was, and so unacquainted with men and things, to come to any certain conclusion who was right and who was wrong," wrote Joseph.[5] Searching the Holy Bible for answers to his growing dilemma led him to a passage in the epistle of James, "If any of you lack wisdom, let him ask of God,

It strikes me so deeply that the vision came to a boy of fourteen. It was important to me, as I painted this scene, to see the face and read the feelings of an innocent boy. When I can visualize his age, the event and the importance of it touch my heart in a powerful way.

that giveth to all men liberally, and upbraideth not; and it shall be given him."[6] In accordance with the directive to ask God, "on the morning of a beautiful, clear day, early in the spring of eighteen hundred and twenty," young Joseph stepped into the woods near his family farm to ask God to unravel the confusion.[7] As he "kneeled down and began to offer up the desires of [his] heart" he was nearly overcome by "the power of some actual being from the unseen world." In this moment of great alarm he exerted "all [his] powers to call upon God to deliver [him] out of the power of this enemy."[8]

"I saw a pillar of light exactly over my head, above the brightness of the sun, which descended gradually until

The First Vision

it fell upon me. It no sooner appeared than I found myself delivered from the enemy. . . . When the light rested upon me I saw two Personages, whose brightness and glory defy all description, standing above me in the air. One of them spake unto me, calling me by name and said, pointing to the other—*This is My Beloved Son. Hear Him!*"[9] As Joseph listened, Jesus Christ told him that the creeds of the contesting Christian sects were "an abomination in his sight," and that the professors of those creeds "teach for doctrines the commandments of men, having a form of godliness, but they deny the power thereof."[10]

The divine answer was definitive. There was no mistaking the Lord's directive. Confidently, the unassuming youth shared glimpses of his manifestation with a local minister. Instead of rejoicing over the boy's vision and the truths he learned from the Son of God, the minister treated his "communication not only lightly, but with great contempt, saying it was all of the devil, that there were no such things as visions or revelations in these days; that all such things had ceased with the apostles."[11] The local clergymen withdrew from the boy and cast aspersions upon him and his family.

Rumors of Joseph's vision spread quickly through the town. Fools derided that which was sacred, and soon contempt and mockery became Joseph's common shadows. "Though I was an obscure boy, only between fourteen and fifteen years of age, and my circumstances in life such as to make a boy of no consequence in the world," Joseph mused, "yet men of high standing would take notice sufficient to excite the public mind against me, and create a bitter persecution."[12]

The opposition caused great sorrow for Joseph.[13] But rather than deny his vision, he firmly stated, "I had actually seen a light, and in the midst of that light I saw two Personages, and they did in reality speak to me; and though I was hated and persecuted for saying that I had seen a vision, yet it was true; . . . I knew it, and I knew that God knew it, and I could not deny it."[14]

Townsfolk labeled him "lazy, intemperate and worthless," "addicted to lying," "a drunkard," and "very quarrelsome."[15] They said, "We knew not of a single individual in this vicinity that puts the least confidence in [his] pretended revelations."[16] When resident Thomas Taylor was asked, "Why didn't they like [young Joseph]?" he answered, "To tell the truth, there was something about him they could not understand; some way he knew more than they did, and it made them mad."[17]

One day as Joseph was standing near Zachariah Blackman's shop, a circuit preacher asked, "Is this boy Holy Joe, whom the angel told that all the religious denominations were believing in false doctrines and none of them was accepted of God?" He was answered, "That's him, ask young Joe when he'll have revealed to him the true doctrine and the fulness of the gospel, so you preachers will know what's in the Bible ain't entirely true."[18] The men laughed.

Joseph endured the mockery, little knowing that there were men living in the United States who would have rejoiced to know of his vision. One such man was Brigham Young, who said, "If I could see the face of a Prophet, such as had lived on the earth in former times, a man that had revelations, to whom the heavens were opened, who knew God and His character, I would freely circumscribe the earth on my hands and knees."[19]

Unfortunately, neither Brigham nor others who would one day hail Joseph as a prophet of God were in Palmyra to defend the rebuffed youth. For Joseph and his family the ever-increasing persecution was the cause of

---

If I could see the face of a Prophet, such as had lived on the earth in former times, . . . I would freely circumscribe the earth on my hands and knees.

—BRIGHAM YOUNG

---

great alarm. Former friends suggested that "not one of the male members of the Smith family were entitled to any credit whatsoever." Joseph and his father were labeled as "entirely destitute of moral character and addicted to vicious habits."[20] William Smith wrote, "We never knew we were bad folks until Joseph told his vision. We were considered respectable till then, but at once people began to circulate falsehoods and stories."[21]

Rumored accounts of Joseph's vision led even clergymen to threaten abuse. "I remember the churchman saying in a very solemn and impressive tone," wrote Martha Cox, "that the very influence the boy carried was the danger they feared for the coming generation, that not only the young men, but all who came in contact with him, would follow him and he must be put down."[22] The mobocratic tone of the preacher's sermon was preceded by a would-be assassin's bullet. One evening as Joseph was returning to his home, "as he was passing through the dooryard, a gun was fired across his pathway."[23]

Adding to his difficulties were Joseph's own actions. He "frequently fell into many foolish errors, and displayed the weakness of youth, and the foibles of human nature."[24] What he had observed as a contradicting message in the preachers' walk and talk was sometimes mirrored in Joseph's own youthful demeanor. However, he confessed, "I have not, neither can it be sustained, in truth, been guilty of wronging or injuring any man or society of men."[25] Yet for a boy who had seen God the Father and Jesus Christ and had suffered "severe persecution at the hands of all classes of men, both religious and irreligious, because I continued to affirm that I had seen a vision," his foolish actions caused him to feel "condemned for [his] weakness and imperfections."[26]

On Sunday evening, September 21, 1823, in the family log cabin in the woods of Palmyra, Joseph supplicated the Lord "for forgiveness of all my sins and follies, and also for a manifestation to me, that I might know of

Traditional paintings of the angel Moroni's visitation to young Joseph depict the seventeen-year-old youth in a room by himself. I chose to paint him in a room with his brothers. After all, his family was in meager circumstances, and thus a separate room for just one son seems improbable. Why did his brothers sleep through the angelic visitation? Is their sleep symbolic of a world failing to awake to heavenly truths? Or does Joseph's solitary wakefulness and response to the angel symbolize his unique role in the Restoration? ♥♥♥♥♥♥♥♥♥♥

my state and standing before him."[27] While calling upon the Lord, "I discovered a light appearing in my room, which continued to increase until the room was lighter than at noonday, when immediately a personage appeared at my bedside, standing in the air, for his feet did not touch the floor."[28] The angelic being "called me by name, and said unto me that he was a messenger sent from the presence of God to me, and that his name was Moroni."[29]

The messenger announced to Joseph that "God had a work for me to do; and that my name should be had for good and evil among all nations, kindreds, and tongues, or that it should be both good and evil spoken

He Called Me by Name

of among all people."[30] The prophesied conflicting repu-tation centered around a book written upon gold plates and a Urim and Thummim prepared "for the purpose of translating the book."[31] As the angel conversed with the boy, "the place where the plates were deposited" was shown him in vision.[32]

This visionary scene and angelic visitation soon ended, and "the room was again left dark."[33] Before dawn the messenger appeared two other times to Joseph and may have "occupied the whole of that night" conversing with the seventeen-year-old youth.[34] Arising after his sleepless night, Joseph walked from the cabin to the fields and began the "necessary labors of the day."[35] He soon discovered his "strength so exhausted as to render [him] entirely unable" to assist his father.[36] While in the act of returning to the cabin, he was again visited by the angel Moroni, who "related unto me all that he had related to me the previous night, and commanded me to go to my father and tell him of the vision and commandments which I had received."[37] In obedience Joseph returned to the fields and told his father. Father Smith assured him of the divine nature of the visitations by stating that "it was of God."[38] Joseph then went directly to the hill he had seen in vision the night before, "a hill of considerable size, and the most elevated of any in the neighborhood," about three miles southeast of the family farm.[39] There, "under a stone of considerable size, lay the plates, deposited in a stone box."[40]

His attempt to take the contents of the box "was for-bidden by the messenger." Joseph was told that "the time for bringing them forth had not yet arrived," and would not "until he had learned to keep the commandments of God—

not only till he was willing but able to do it."[41]

Four years would pass before Joseph would receive the plates and the Urim and Thummim. During those years his family listened to his recitation of heavenly truths. "He would describe the ancient inhabitants of this continent, their dress, mode of traveling, and the animals upon which they rode; their cities, their buildings, with every particu-lar; their mode of warfare; and also their religious worship. This he would do with as much ease, seemingly, as if he had spent his whole life among them," said his mother.[42] "I presume our family presented an aspect as singular as any that ever lived upon the face of the earth," she wrote, "—all seated in a circle, father, mother, sons and daugh-ters, and giving the most profound attention to a boy."[43]

 H E   R E A S O N for their attentiveness was the Smiths' "implicit confidence in . . . Joseph concerning his vision and the knowledge he thereby obtained con-cerning the plates."[44] When his brother William was asked, "Did you not doubt Joseph's testimony sometimes?" he replied, "No[,] we all had implicit confidence in what he said. He was a truthful boy. Father and Mother believed him; why should not the children? . . . No sir, we never doubted his word for a minute."[45] The family believed in Joseph and readily came to his defense. One evening as Joseph entered the home, Joseph, Sr., inquired, "Joseph, why are you so late? has anything happened to you? we have been much distressed about you these three hours." Joseph said, "I have taken the severest chastisement that I

have ever had in my life." Father Smith, surmising that the mob element in Palmyra was harassing his son, rejoined, "I would like to know what business anybody has to find fault with you!" Joseph countered, "Stop, father, stop, it was the angel of the Lord." The angelic messenger told him that he "had not been engaged enough in the work of the Lord; that the time had come for the record to be brought forth; and that I must be up and doing and set myself about the things which God had commanded me to do."[46]

As Joseph prepared himself to receive the plates and interpreters, he charged his family to never mention outside of the family circle the heavenly truths he shared; for "the world was so wicked that when they came to a knowledge of these things they would try to take our lives."[47] Yet despite his family's promises, news of Joseph's angelic visitations and preparations spread to the community. "False reports, misrepresentations, and base slanders flew, as if upon the wings of the wind in every direction."[48] Neighbors strained to hear fanciful accounts and retorted with mockery and ridicule. The family remained calm through the abuse. Mother Smith wrote, "Truly ours was a happy family, although persecuted by the preachers, who declared there was no more vision, the canon of scripture was full, and no more revelation was needed."[49] The Smiths "were now confirmed in the opinion that God was about to bring to light something upon which we could stay our minds, or that would give us a more perfect knowledge of the plan of salvation and the redemption of the human family. This caused us greatly to rejoice, the sweetest union and happiness pervaded our house, and tranquility reigned in our midst."[50]

Notes

1. See Joseph Smith–History 1:21.

2. JS–H 1:5.

3. JS–H 1:5.

4. Alexander Neibaur's recording of Joseph Smith's testimony, 24 May 1844, as cited in Milton V. Backman Jr., *Joseph Smith's First Vision* (Salt Lake City: Bookcraft, 1971), p. 177.

5. *History of The Church of Jesus Christ of Latter-day Saints,* ed. B. H. Roberts (Salt Lake City: Deseret Book Co., 1932), 1:3–4; JS–H 1:8.

6. James 1:5.

7. JS–H 1:14.

8. JS–H 1:15–16.

9. JS–H 1:16–17.

10. JS–H 1:19.

11. JS–H 1:21.

12. JS–H 1:22.

13. See JS–H 1:23.

14. JS–H 1:25.

15. Eber D. Howe, *Mormonism Unvailed* (Painesville, Ohio: E. D. Howe, 1834), pp. 249, 259.

16. Ibid., p. 248.

17. *The Juvenile Instructor* 17 (1 October 1882): 302.

18. Pomeroy Tucker, *Origin, Rise, and Progress of Mormonism: Biography of its founders and history of its church: personal remembrances and historical collections hitherto unwritten* (New York: D. Appleton and Co., 1867), p. 28.

19. In JD 4:104.

20. Howe, *Mormonism Unvailed,* pp. 248–61.

21. *The Deseret Evening News,* 20 January 1894.

22. "Stories from the Notebook of Martha Cox, Grandmother of Fern Cox Anderson," as cited in Ivan J. Barrett, *Young Joseph* (n.p.: RIC

Publishing, 1981), p. 54.

23. Smith, *History of Joseph Smith,* p. 67.

24. JS–H 1:28.

25. *Latter-day Saints' Messenger and Advocate,* December 1834, p. 40.

26. JS–H 1:27, 29.

27. JS–H 1:29.

28. JS–H 1:30.

29. JS–H 1:33.

30. Ibid.

31. JS–H 1:35.

32. JS–H 1:42.

33. JS–H 1:43.

34. JS–H 1:47.

35. JS–H 1:48.

36. Ibid.

37. JS–H 1:49.

38. JS–H 1:50.

39. JS–H 1:51.

40. Ibid.

41. *History of the Church* 1:16; JS–H 1:53; Smith, *History of Joseph Smith,* p. 81.

42. Smith, *History of Joseph Smith,* p. 83.

43. Ibid., p. 82.

44. Blue Book, 0127-No. 9871, LDS Church Archives, as cited in Barrett, *Young Joseph,* pp. 70–71.

45. "Journal History of the Church," manuscript copy, 20 January 1894, as cited in Barrett, *Young Joseph,* p. 73.

46. Smith, *History of Joseph Smith,* p. 100.

47. Ibid., p. 82.

48. Orson Pratt, *An Interesting Account of Several Remarkable Visions* (1842), p. 15.

49. Wandle Mace Autobiography, typescript, Special Collections, Harold B. Lee Library, Brigham Young University, Provo, Utah, p. 47.

50. Smith, *History of Joseph Smith,* pp. 82–83.

CHAPTER THREE

F T H E many events that occurred during the four years that lapsed between the 1823 visitation of the angel Moroni and Joseph's receiving the gold plates, no event is more publicized than his brief encounter with treasure hunting. The hours of cutting timber and digging wells, the untimely death of his brother Alvin, and the construction of a new home are only faint remembrances of the preparatory years because the labels "treasure hunter"

and "money digger" are publicly heralded. These disparaging titles, although just two in a litany of his enemies' derogatory terms for Joseph, cast doubts on his explanation of the coming forth of the Book of Mormon. His account of an angel, the plates, and the Urim and Thummim becomes clouded, if not absurd, when coupled with an

"On account of having heard that [Joseph] possessed certain means by which he could discern things invisible to the natural eye," he was hired to dig for the lost silver mine in the Oquago Mountain at Harmony, Pennsylvania.[1] Although Joseph "endeavored to divert [his employer] from his vain pursuit," he accepted the

I cannot study the life of Joseph Smith without wondering about Emma. I have come to love and respect Joseph's beloved wife, of whom the Lord said, "Thou art an elect lady, whom I have called." (D&C 25:3.) *✏ ✏ ✏* **Emma Smith has probably been judged and misjudged more than any other individual in our church's history. It amazes me that even the mention of her name continues to stir such varied emotions. I often wish that we had more information about Emma and Joseph's life together, but when I think of how their lives are already open to such scrutiny, I am silently pleased for Emma that we do not.** *✏ ✏ ✏*

announcement that Joseph was a "money digger"; and his declarations then smack of typical widespread imaginations that emerged in nineteenth-century New York.

It is common knowledge that by the 1820s men residing in and around Palmyra employed magic to search for hidden treasures by unorthodox means. Upright citizens and greedy speculators alike believed that great treasures, even a legendary lost Spanish silver mine, were concealed in the earth. Men scoured the land looking for hidden wealth. Their insatiable desire for riches caused them to abandon farm labor for a crazed and frenzied search.

terms of employment and in October 1825 journeyed to Harmony to commence digging.[2] "I continued to work for nearly a month, without success in [my] undertaking, and finally I prevailed with the [employer] to cease digging," wrote Joseph.[3] The digging stopped on November 17, 1825, about one month after it began.

The unfruitful dig unwittingly brought Joseph closer to the matrimonial altar. As a hired hand for treasure speculators, he boarded with the Isaac Hale family and, as he later recorded, "first saw my wife (his daughter), Emma Hale."[4] Emma, at that time a schoolteacher, stood about five feet nine inches tall, had dark hair and

An Elect Lady

More Than Friends

brown eyes, and was described as "well turned, of excellent form . . . with splendid physical development."[5]

The happiness of meeting his future bride was tempered by the cold reception of Emma's father. Joseph attributed the animosity to "my continuing to assert that I had seen a vision."[6] His adherence to the reality of the vision and the visitations of the angel Moroni evoked prejudice

her choice happy than Miss Emma Hale . . . whom he had been extremely fond of since his first introduction to her."[9]

Emma was married to Joseph on January 18, 1827, in South Bainbridge, New York, by Squire Tarbell. "I had no intention of marrying when I left home," Emma wrote, "but . . . [Joseph] urged me to marry him, and preferring to marry him to any other man I knew, I consented."[10]

 **I sorrowed with Emma as I read that she left her family under difficult circumstances to marry the man she loved. Emma was loved by Joseph and also by his family, especially Mother Smith. She embraced and welcomed Emma as a daughter and willingly cared for her during times of illness. Emma returned her love by comforting Mother Smith in her later years. I think these women rejoiced that they were more than friends—bound together eternally as mother and daughter.** ♥ ♥ ♥ ♥ ♥ ♥ ♥ ♥ ♥

and persecution that "followed me, and my wife's father's family were very much opposed to our being married."[7]

Isaac Hale wrote of Joseph's courting his daughter, "Smith made several visits at my house, and at length asked my consent to his marrying my daughter Emma. This I refused. . . . He then left the place."[8] Joseph returned to Palmyra but could not forget his feelings for Emma. "He had come to the conclusion of getting married," wrote Mother Smith. "He thought that no young woman that he ever was acquainted with was better calculated to render the man of

When her father learned of the marriage, he claimed that his 22-year-old daughter had been abducted by a "careless young man, not very well educated."[11]

Knowing of Hale's opposition to the marriage, Joseph took his bride to Palmyra where his mother had "put [her] house in order for the reception of [her] son's bride."[12] Emma was welcomed by the Smiths and recognized by them for her unselfish service: "whatever her hands found to do, she did with her might, until so far beyond her strength that she brought upon herself a heavy fit of sickness."[13] Yet Emma did not complain. "I have never seen a woman in my life, who would endure every species of fatigue and hardship, from month to month, and from year to year," wrote Mother Smith, "with that unflinching courage, zeal, and patience, which she has ever done."[14]

Perhaps for her Christian service, or by divine appointment, Emma was privileged to ride beside Joseph on his journey to the Hill Cumorah after midnight on

off; but that if I would use all my endeavors to preserve them, . . . they should be protected."[16]

When he and Emma returned home with news of the unearthed treasure, the Smith household rejoiced. They listened to Joseph's caution to keep secret their joy, but "Satan had now stirred up the hearts of those who had gotten a hint of the matter . . . to search into it and make every possible move towards thwarting the pur-

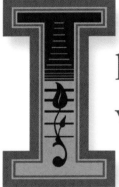 have never seen a woman . . . who woul with that unflinching courage, zeal, an

September 22, 1827. Joseph climbed the hill to the place where the plates were deposited while Emma waited in the wagon, and Mother Smith prayed at home, "for the anxiety of my mind would not permit me to sleep. . . . [I] feared lest Joseph might meet with another disappointment."[15] Disappointment was not to be his in 1827. "Having gone as usual . . . to the place where [the plates] were deposited," Joseph was met by "the same heavenly messenger [who] delivered [the plates] up to me with this charge: that I should be responsible for them; that if I should let them go carelessly, or through any neglect of mine, I should be cut

poses of the Almighty."[17] As word of gold treasure spread in Palmyra from house to house, curiosity, unseemly efforts, and assailants tried to take what they called "Joe Smith's Gold Bible." Cash and property were offered for a glimpse of the plates. When Joseph refused, schemes were contrived to snatch the revealed treasure. The mob element shouted, "We will have them plates in spite of Joe Smith or all the devils in hell."[18]

Keeping the plates safe and out of sight proved difficult for Joseph. A birch log, hearthstones, floorboards, flax, and a barrel of beans were used to hide the plates and keep thieves at bay. But there was little stopping mobocracy from mushrooming in Palmyra. As the frenzy over the "Gold Bible" mounted, Joseph "was under the necessity of leaving" the area.[19] He turned to his father-in-law, Isaac Hale, in Harmony, Pennsylvania, for refuge from the treasure hunters.

Hale initially welcomed his daughter and son-in-law into his home in the winter of 1827, and there Joseph "com-

translation and scribing of the Book of Mormon that took place in the house.

The plates "lay in a box under our bed for months," said Emma, "but I never felt at liberty to look at them."[22] They were occasionally on a table in the living room "wrapped in a small linen table cloth, which I had given him to fold them in. I once felt of the plates, as they thus lay on the table, tracing their outline and shape. They seemed

ndure every species of fatigue and hardship . . . patience, which [Emma] has ever done.

—LUCY MACK SMITH

menced copying the characters off the plates."[20] However, when Hale discovered that Joseph had a chest containing secret contents, hospitality ended. Hale, like the treasure hunters of Palmyra, "was determined to see" the plates.[21] Joseph's refusal deepened the family rift and led to his removal from the Hale home to a small farmhouse nearby.

For the next two and a half years the farmhouse was the residence of Joseph and Emma. During those years Emma gave birth to a son, only to lose him a few hours later, and the manuscript pages of the book of Lehi were lost. These tragedies were perhaps tempered by the

to be pliable like thick paper, and would rustle with a metallic sound when the edges were moved by the thumb, as one does sometimes thumb the edges of a book."[23]

Emma scribed a portion of the Book of Mormon translation that came from those plates and said of her experience, "The Book of Mormon is of divine authenticity—I have not the slightest doubt of it. I am satisfied that no man could have dictated the writing of the manuscripts unless he was inspired; for, when acting as his scribe, [he] would dictate to me hour after hour; and when returning after meals, or after interruptions, he would at once begin where he had left off, without either seeing the manuscript or having any portion of it read to him. This was a usual thing for him to do. It would have been improbable that a learned man could do this; and, for one so ignorant and unlearned as he was, it was simply impossible."[24]

upon [the American] continent," he had questions about authority to "administer the ordinances of the gospel."[26] Seeking an answer, he and Oliver "went into the woods to pray and inquire of the Lord respecting baptism for the remission of sins, that we found mentioned in the transla-

 **I am awed by the magnitude of this sacred event. For thousands of years, the world had been shrouded in darkness. Christ's church was no longer upon the earth, yet righteous men and women still struggled to find it.** ❧❧ **I think how hard it is for me as a parent when my children want something I cannot give them. Imagine the joy in heaven as our Heavenly Father, with the restoration of the Melchizedek Priesthood, answered in one moment millions of prayers offered over thousands of years. With the hands of Peter, James, and John came hope to a hopeless world.**

The principal scribe of the Book of Mormon, Oliver Cowdery, testified, "These were days never to be forgotten—to sit under the sound of a voice dictated by the inspiration of heaven, awakened the utmost gratitude of this bosom. Day after day I continued, uninterrupted, to write from his mouth, as he translated, with the Urim and Thummim . . . the history, or record, called 'The book of Mormon.'"[25]

While Joseph was translating "the account given of the Savior's ministry to the remnant of the seed of Jacob,

tion of the plates."[27] While praying on May 15, 1829, near the timber-lined Susquehanna River, "a messenger from heaven descended in a cloud of light, and having laid his hands upon us, he ordained us, saying: *Upon you my fellow servants, in the name of Messiah, I confer the Priesthood of Aaron, which holds the keys of the ministering of angels, and of the gospel of repentance, and of baptism by immersion for the remission of sins; and this shall never be taken again from the earth until the sons of Levi do offer again an offering unto the Lord in righteousness.*"[28]

The Restoration of the Melchizedek Priesthood

The messenger was the prophet John, known in the New Testament as John the Baptist. He commanded Joseph and Oliver "to go and be baptized, and gave us directions that I should baptize Oliver Cowdery, and that afterwards he should baptize me."[29] Upon rising from the watery baptism, Joseph "prophesied concerning the rise of this church, and many other things connected with the Church, and this generation of the children of men."[30]

John the Baptist promised that the priesthood of Melchizedek "would in due time be conferred on us," said Joseph.[31] In answer to another prayer, three ancient apostles—Peter, James, and John—restored the Melchizedek Priesthood and the keys of the apostleship to Joseph and Oliver.[32] "I was also present with Joseph," wrote Oliver of this sacred occasion, "when the higher or Melchizedek Priesthood was conferred by holy angels from on high. This Priesthood we then conferred on each other, by the will and commandment of God."[33]

The priesthood brought added dimension to the translation process. "Our minds being now enlightened," wrote Joseph, "we began to have the scriptures laid open to our understandings, and the true meaning and intention of their more mysterious passages revealed unto us in a manner which we never could attain to previously, nor ever before had thought of."[34] Yet Joseph felt "forced to keep secret" the truths he was learning because of mounting persecution in Harmony—"and this, too, by professors of religion."[35]

Vile rumors were spreading, and many were threatening evil against Joseph "in order to prevent the work of God from going forth to the world."[36] Fearing for the Book of Mormon manuscript as much as for their own lives, in May 1829 Joseph abandoned the farmhouse in Harmony and, with Oliver, fled to the home of Peter Whitmer, Sr., in Fayette, New York, for what they hoped would be tranquility and safety. Emma soon joined them, and the translation quickly resumed. Joseph "worked from morning till night."[37]

As the work neared completion, Peter Whitmer's son David noted an interesting episode involving

*O*ur minds being now enlightened, we began to have the scriptures laid open to our understanding, and the true meaning and intention of their more mysterious passages revealed unto us.

contention between Joseph and his wife: "One morning when [Joseph] was getting ready to continue the translation, something went wrong about the house and he was put out about it. Something that Emma, his wife, had done. Oliver and I went up stairs, and Joseph came up soon after to continue the translation, but he could not do anything. He could not translate a single syllable. He went down stairs, out into the orchard and made supplication to the Lord; was gone about an hour—came back to the house, asked Emma's forgiveness and then came up stairs where we were and the translation went on all right."[38]

It was during this time that the Lord saw fit to allow three of Joseph's close associates—Oliver Cowdery, David Whitmer, and Martin Harris—to see the golden plates for themselves and become witnesses that the ancient scriptures had been "translated by the gift and power of God, for his voice hath declared it unto us; Wherefore we know of a surety that the work is true."[39]

After seeing the sacred record, the three witnesses who were shown the plates by the angel testified so eloquently of the truthfulness of Joseph's words that he said to his parents, "Father, mother, you do not know how happy I am: the Lord has now caused the plates to be shown to three more besides myself. . . . They will have to bear witness to the truth of what I have said, . . . and I feel as if I was relieved of a burden which was almost too heavy for me to bear, and it rejoices my soul, that I am not any longer to be entirely alone in the world."[40]

Notes

1. Smith, *History of Joseph Smith,* pp. 91–92.

2. Ibid., p. 92.

3. JS–H 1:56.

4. JS–H 1:57.

5. Inez A. Kennedy, *Recollections of the Pioneers of Lee County* (Dixon, Illinois: n.p., 1893), p. 96, as cited in Linda King Newell and Valeen Tippetts Avery, *Mormon Enigma: Emma Hale Smith* (New York: Doubleday, 1984), p. 1.

6. *HC* 1:17.

7. JS–H 1:58.

8. Statement of Isaac Hale, reprinted in Emily C. Blackman, *History of Susquehanna County, Pennsylvania* (Philadelphia: Claxton, Remsen, and Haffelfinger, 1873), p. 578, as cited in Susan Easton Black, "Isaac Hale: Antagonist of Joseph Smith," *Regional Studies in Latter-day Saint Church History: New York* (Provo, Utah: Department of Church History and Doctrine, Brigham Young University, 1992), p. 100.

9. Smith, "Preliminary Manuscript," as cited in Newell and Avery, *Mormon Enigma,* p. 19.

10. "Last Testimony of Sister Emma," *The Saints' Herald* 26 (1 October 1879): 289–90, as cited in Milton V. Backman, Jr., *Eyewitness Accounts of the Restoration* (Orem, Utah: Grandin Book Co., 1983), p. 54.

11. Blackman, *History of Susquehanna County, Pennsylvania,* p. 578.

12. Smith, *History of Joseph Smith,* p. 94.

13. Ibid., p. 190.

14. Ibid., pp. 190–91.

15. Ibid., p. 102.

16. JS–H 1:59.

17. Smith, *History of Joseph Smith,* p. 105.

18. Ibid., 106.

19. JS–H 1:61.

20. JS–H 1:62.

21. *The Susquehanna Register* (Montrose, Pennsylvania), 1 May 1834, as cited in Porter, New York Dissertation, p. 133.

22. Interview of Emma Smith Bidamon by Nels Madson and Parley P. Pratt, Jr., 1877, LDS Church Archives.

23. "Last Testimony of Sister Emma," p. 290.

24. Ibid.

25. *Messenger and Advocate,* October 1834, p. 14.

26. *Messenger and Advocate,* October 1834, p. 15, as cited in Bushman, *Joseph Smith and the Beginnings of Mormonism* (Urbana and Chicago: University of Illinois Press, 1984), p. 100.

27. JS–H 1:68.

28. JS–H 1:68–69.

29. JS–H 1:70.

30. *HC* 1:42.

31. JS–H 1:72.

32. See D&C 27:12.

33. Preston Nibley, *Witnesses of the Book of Mormon* (Salt Lake City: Stevens and Wallis, 1946), p. 48.

34. JS–H 1:74.

35. JS–H 1:74–75.

36. Smith, *History of Joseph Smith,* p. 147.

37. *Deseret Evening News,* 25 March 1884, as cited in Porter, New York Dissertation, p. 238.

38. "Letter from Elder W. H. Kelley, *Saints' Herald,* 1 March 1882, p. 68.

39. Introduction, Book of Mormon.

40. Smith, *History of Joseph Smith,* p. 152.

CHAPTER FOUR

LTHOUGH the *Freeman* newspaper mistakenly reported that the "'Golden Bible' was almost invariably treated as it should have been—with contempt," as soon as the Book of Mormon was published it set "the country in an uproar."[1] Friends and strangers took opposing sides for or against what Joseph was calling the word of God. Joseph testified that "the Book of Mormon was the most correct of any book on earth, and the keystone of our religion, and a man would get nearer to God by abiding by its precepts, than by any other book."[2]

A few, like Joseph's sister Katherine, were convinced of its truthfulness: "Many times when I have read its sacred pages, I have wept like a child, while the Spirit has borne witness with my spirit of its truth."[3] Editors of the *Rochester Daily Advertiser* and *Horn of the Green Mountains* labeled it "Blasphemy" and "Fanaticism." Reporters from the *Rochester Daily Advertiser* printed that a "viler imposition was never practiced. It is an evidence of fraud, blasphemy, and credulity, shocking both to Christians and Moralists."[4]

The anti-Mormon sentiment did not prevent seekers or the curious from reading the Book of Mormon and visiting Joseph, "some for the sake of finding the truth [and] others for the purpose of putting hard questions, and trying to confound."[5] Answers to their queries led many to believe that Joseph Smith was a prophet. Believers longed for the day when the Lord's promise, "If this generation harden not their hearts, I will establish my church among them," would be fulfilled.[6] They waited for the Lord to organize his church "upon the foundation of my gospel and my rock, [and] the gates of hell shall not prevail."[7]

About fifty believers met in obedience to revelation on Tues-day, April 6, 1830, in the Peter Whitmer, Sr., log cabin in Fayette, New York, in what became the first organizational meeting of The Church of Jesus Christ of Latter-day Saints. The meeting was opened with prayer, emblems of the Savior's sacrifice were blessed and passed, and "the Holy Ghost was poured out upon us to a very great degree—some prophesied, whilst we all praised the Lord, and rejoiced exceedingly."[8] Joseph was acknowledged as "a seer, a translator, a prophet, an apostle of Jesus Christ, an elder of the church through the will of God the Father, and the grace of your Lord Jesus Christ."[9]

After the meeting, several of those who attended

wanted to paint the organization of the Church of Jesus Christ. I thought of six men signing a charter, but for me that particular image did not capture the significance of that April day. It was when I read of the baptism of Joseph's father that I knew what I wanted to paint—the joy of a son at his father's acceptance of truth. ❧ ❧ ❧

expressed a desire to be baptized. Among their number were Father and Mother Smith, "to my great joy and consolation," wrote Joseph.[10] After Father Smith was baptized by his son, Joseph clasped him by the hand and exclaimed, "Praise to my God! that I lived to see my own father baptized into the true Church of Jesus Christ!"[11]

When members of Reverend Diedrich Willers's pastorate presented themselves for baptism into the fledgling church, the reverend mocked the upstart religion and its founder, saying, "The greatest imposter of our times in the field of religion is no doubt a certain Joseph Smith. . . .

Praise to My God

This new sect should not cause the Christian Church great astonishment. The past centuries have also had religious off-shoots. . . . They have all been absorbed in the Sea of the Past and marked with the stamp of oblivion. This will also be the lot of the Mormonites, and, I hope, while it is still in the bud."[12] But such was not to be. The Church is "like to a grain of mustard seed, which a man took, and sowed in his field: . . . when it is grown, it is the greatest among herbs."[13]

Vain attempts to stop Mormonism failed again and again. When sectarian ministers instigated a mob to destroy a dam across a stream to prevent further baptisms, the dam was rebuilt and believers immersed in baptismal covenants. When a mob, "raging with anger, and apparently determined to commit violence," surrounded a home where Joseph was visiting, he escaped "by the exercise of great prudence . . . and reliance in our heavenly Father."[14]

When Joseph was charged with "being a disorderly person, of setting the country in an uproar by preaching the Book of Mormon," a court of law was held to determine his guilt. Spectators filled the courtroom to capacity and expected a verdict of guilty. To their dismay Joseph was acquitted. However, before he could leave the courtroom another warrant was issued for his arrest. The constable "took me to a tavern, and gathered in a number of men, who used every means to abuse, ridicule and insult me," said Joseph. "They spit upon me, pointed their fingers at me, saying, 'Prophesy, prophesy!'" Yet despite the abuse he was acquitted at the second trial. His lawyers "put to silence their opponents, and convince[d] the court that I was innocent. They spoke like men inspired of God," said Joseph.[15]

In reflecting upon the failure of his enemies to stop Mormonism, Joseph mused, "We feared not our opponents, knowing that we had both truth and righteousness on our side. . . . We had the doctrines of Christ, and abided in them."[16] The Prophet and the newly baptized converts moved forward in ways they had not thought possible before the organization of the Church. Those who once feared to speak now opened their mouths to "declare repentance" and bring other "souls unto [Christ]."[17] "Many opened their houses to us," said Joseph. "Our meetings were well attended, and many began to pray fervently to Almighty God, that He would give them wisdom to understand the truth."[18]

Among those who understood and defended Mormonism were Joseph Smith's family. Father Smith endured the privations of exposure and jail rather than burn one copy of the Book of Mormon. When his son Samuel came to visit him after four days of confinement, Father Smith said, "Immediately after I left your mother, the men by whom I was taken commenced using every possible argument to induce me to renounce the Book of Mormon, saying, 'how much better it would be for you to deny that silly thing, than to be disgraced and imprisoned, when you might . . . escape this.' . . . I thought to myself, I was not the first man who had been imprisoned for the truth's sake; and when I should meet Paul in the Paradise of God, I could tell him that I, too, had been in bonds for the Gospel which he had preached."[19]

Mother Smith was also bold in her testimony of the Book of Mormon and her son's role in translating the word of God. In answer to a Presbyterian pastor's remark, "And you are the mother of that poor, foolish, silly boy, Joe Smith, who pretended to translate the Book of Mormon," Lucy replied, "I am, sir, the mother of Joseph Smith; but why do you apply to him such epithets as those?" The reverend retorted, "Because that he should imagine he was going to break down all other churches with that simple 'Mormon' book."

"Did you ever read that book?" she inquired.

"No," said he, "it is beneath my notice."

"But," rejoined Mother Smith, "the Scriptures say, 'prove all things'; and, now, sir, let me tell you boldly, that that book contains the everlasting gospel, and it was written for the salvation of your soul, by the gift and power of the Holy Ghost." "Pooh," said the minister, "nonsense—I am not afraid of any member of my church being led astray by such stuff; they have too much intelligence."[20] Less than three years later, a third of his congregation had joined the Church.

The Smiths shared the gospel with friends, pastors, congregations, and strangers, who in turn shared the gospel message with near neighbors and distant relatives.

Young and old, rich and poor, farmer and educator stopped to listen. Among the listeners was Warren Foote: "I had no faith in the religious teachings of the various sects, and their revivals and shouting meetings, made no serious impressions on my mind. I could not believe that the Church of Christ was divided into creeds and sects, and I resolved that I would not have anything to do with any of them, but frequently prayed to the Lord in secret to guide me in the right way."[21] After comparing the Book of Mormon with the Bible, Foote joined with Mormonism.

Early converts like Warren Foote proclaimed the truthfulness of the Book of Mormon and professed their witness that Joseph Smith was a prophet of God.

Joseph humbly acknowledged his prophetic calling, but assured his followers, "I am like a huge, rough stone rolling down from a high mountain; and the only polishing I get is when some corner gets rubbed off . . . all hell knocking off a corner here and a corner there. Thus I will become a smooth and polished shaft in the quiver of the Almighty."[22] Like other early believers the young prophet needed refining.

Notes

1. Richard L. Bushman, *Joseph Smith and the Beginnings of Mormonism* (Chicago: University of Illinois Press, 1984), p. 111; *HC* 1:88.

2. *HC* 4:461.

3. Katherine Salisbury, "Dear Sisters." *Saints' Herald* 33 (1 May 1886): 260.

4. Bushman, *Joseph Smith and the Beginnings of Mormonism,* pp. 111–12.

5. *HC* 1:59.

6. D&C 10:53.

7. D&C 18:5.

8. *HC* 1:78.

9. D&C 21:1.

10. *HC* 1:79.

11. Smith, *History of Joseph Smith,* p. 168.

12. "Church Book of the Reformed Church of Christ in Fayette Township, Seneca County in State of New York, 1833," as cited in Larry C.

Porter, Milton V. Backman Jr., and Susan Easton Black, eds., *Regional Studies in Latter-day Saint Church History: New York* (Provo, Ut.: Department of Church History and Doctrine, Brigham Young University, 1992), p. 161.

13. Matthew 13:31–32.

14. *HC* 1:88.

15. *HC* 1:88–94.

16. *HC* 1:84.

17. D&C 15:6.

18. *HC* 1:84, 51, 81.

19. Smith, *History of Joseph Smith,* p. 185.

20. Ibid., pp. 215–16.

21. Andrew Jenson, *Latter-day Saint Biographical Encyclopedia,* 4 vols. (Salt Lake City: Deseret News, 1901–36), 1:376.

22. *HC* 5:401.

CHAPTER FIVE

EARLY missionaries journeyed through western New York with carpetbags filled with copies of the Book of Mormon, which they shared with strangers. To share the books with native Americans, these missionaries trekked through the extensive woodlands of the north-east, and by October 1830 they were in the Ohio wilderness.  The religious stir created by their message in small villages and towns near the agrarian community of

Kirtland, Ohio, is legendary. "The people thronged us night and day," wrote missionary Parley P. Pratt, "insomuch that we had no time for rest or retirement."[1] About one hundred and thirty persons were baptized before the missionaries

**hero is someone you look up to, admire, and even want to emulate. Joseph Smith was a hero for the children. Why did they follow him, want to be with him and even be like him? I think it has something to do with the Savior's invitation, "Come, follow me." Joseph followed Jesus Christ, and the children recognized in him Christlike qualities.**

bid farewell and continued their journey to the frontier.

Left without seasoned members to guide their religious zeal, the new converts soon found their enthusiasm overshadowed their gospel understanding. Unknowingly, they accepted misguided visions and spurious revelations as doctrines from God. Abnormal physical gyrations and speaking in unfamiliar tongues were touted as evidences of God's approval of their spirituality. Failure to distinguish between the powers of light and the powers of darkness and "strange notions and false spirits" led to open conflicts between members.[2]

The newly baptized members wanted answers to their emerging religious troubles and prayed fervently that the Lord would send the Prophet Joseph to Kirtland to solve their contentions. Their prayers were answered in a revelation given to Joseph in December 1830. In the revelation he was commanded to gather the Saints, meaning his followers, out of western New York "because of the enemy and for your sakes."[3] In obedience to the revelation, the New York Saints sold their houses, out-dwellings, and other possessions to migrate to Ohio. "As might be expected, we were obliged to make great sacrifices of our property," wrote Newel Knight of Colesville, New York.[4] Peter Whitmer sold his Fayette acreage and log cabin for $2,200, but others were less fortunate. The *Painesville Telegraph* announced that in spite of the varying economic circumstances of Joseph's followers, "about two hundred men, women and children, of the deluded followers of Jo Smith's Bible speculation, have arrived on our coast . . . from New-York."[5]

As one journalist observed the Mormon migration, he was led to believe the "whole world" was centering in rural Kirtland: "They came . . . in every conceivable manner, some with horses, oxen, and vehicles rough and rude, while others had walked all or part of the distance. The future 'City of the Saints' appeared like one besieged. Every available house, shop, hut, or barn was filled to its utmost capacity. Even boxes were roughly extemporized and used for shelter until something more permanent could be secured."[6]

In early February 1831, twenty-five-year-old Joseph and his wife of four years, Emma, arrived in Kirtland by

Heroes Like Joseph

Go with Me to Cumorah

sleigh. As Joseph stepped from the sleigh, he walked directly up the steps of the Gilbert and Whitney mercantile store and said, "Newel K. Whitney! Thou art the man!" Whitney, a recent Mormon convert, replied, "You have the advantage of me. I could not call you by name as you have me." Joseph said, "I am Joseph the Prophet. You've prayed me here, now what do you want of me?"[7]

The answer was apparent—each new convert wanted to learn the truths of the gospel from the Lord's

"gold bible" and Joseph's family as a "gang of money diggers."[10] They took unkindly to "false reports, lies, and foolish stories," as they did to individuals who found fault with Joseph.[11] Newly baptized Joseph Wakefield was shunned by Mormon society when it was reported that "while he was a guest in the house of Joseph Smith, he had absolutely seen the Prophet come down from the room where he was engaged in translating the word of God, and actually go to playing with the children! This

 s Joseph prepared to leave New York, perhaps he reflected on the glorious event at the Sacred Grove and receiving the plates at the Hill Cumorah. With only glimpses ahead of future revelations in Ohio, he did not hesitate to leave his surroundings to obey the Lord's command. The twenty-five-year-old Joseph ventured forth with courage. As he did, so must I do in order to enjoy the blessings of God.

prophet. They listened intently as Joseph taught them to discern the Spirit of the Lord and to keep the commandments of God. "I have never saw anything like it on the earth," said Mary Elizabeth Rollins; "I could not take my eyes off him."[8] Brigham Young said, "What a delight it was to hear brother Joseph talk upon the great principles of eternity; he would bring them down to the capacity of a child, and he would unite heaven with earth."[9]

The Saints loved Joseph and grimaced when the Ohio newspapers referred to the Book of Mormon as the

convinced him that the Prophet was not a man of God, and that the work was false."[12]

To a man who loudly railed against Joseph, "Woe! woe! unto the inhabitants of this place," Brigham Young didn't mince words. "I put my pants and shoes on, took my cow-hide, went out, and laying hold of him, jerked him round, and assured him that if he did not stop his noise and let the people enjoy their sleep without interruption, I would cow-hide him on the spot, for we had the Lord's Prophet right here, and we did not want the

Brother Joseph's Revenge

This painting illustrates the love Joseph had for children and the respectful love they returned. The Prophet was not too busy to interact with even the smallest members of his following. I most want you to see how comfortable the children are with the Prophet. I like to think that because they instinctively knew his love and concern for him, they had no fear of him. ✒ It is easy to remember the angel Moroni's visit, the First Vision, and the translation of the Book of Mormon. What we forget is that those events did not occupy every minute of Joseph's life. He knew the value of "loosening the bow," as evidenced by many anecdotes related by those who knew him. ✒ The children *could* have started this water fight, but I can almost guarantee who really did! ✒

Devil's prophet yelling round the streets."[13]

From the hostile to the hopeful, curiosity seekers came to Kirtland to meet the man many were calling the Lord's prophet. Of the many people Joseph met, fifty-three-year-old John Johnson and his wife, Elsa, from Hiram, were among the most interesting. As they

Could you gaze into heaven five minutes, you would know more than you would by reading all that ever was written. . . .

conversed with Joseph on the godly gifts that had been conferred during Christ's ministry, one of the visitors exclaimed, "Here is Mrs. Johnson with a lame arm; has God given any power to man now on the earth to cure her?" Joseph, taking Elsa's hand, proclaimed, "Woman, in the name of the Lord Jesus Christ I command thee to be whole."[14] Immediately Elsa raised her arm, even

though she had been afflicted by chronic rheumatism in her shoulder. By accounts of both believers and non-believers, she was thereafter able to do even heavy scrubbing without difficulty or pain.

The miracle for Elsa led directly to the baptism of the Johnsons and a cordial invitation from them for Joseph to accept their hospitality. "On the 12th of September [1831], I removed with my family to the township of Hiram, and commenced living with John Johnson."[15] Joseph's family consisted of his wife, Emma, and the six-month-old twins of John Murdock, whom Joseph and Emma were rearing as their own.

From the time of their arrival at the farmhouse in Hiram "until the forepart of October, [Joseph] did little more than prepare to re-commence the translation of the Bible."[16] When the preparation period ended, "I renewed my work on the translation of the Scriptures."[17] It soon became apparent to him that "many important points touching the salvation of man, had been taken from the Bible, or lost before it was compiled."[18]

The missing scriptural passages were revealed to Joseph by the Lord. "Could you gaze into heaven five minutes, you would know more than you would by reading all that ever was written on the subject," he said.[19] For example, as he was translating John 5:29, Joseph and his scribe, Sidney Rigdon, saw in vision God the Father and His Son Jesus Christ and testified, "After the many testimonies which have been given of him, this is the testimony, last of all, which we give of him: That he lives! For we saw him, even on the right hand of God; and we heard the voice bearing record that he is the Only Begotten of the Father."[20]

I am grateful for the light and truth revealed through
a modern prophet. The plain and precious
missing truths of biblical text needed to be restored,
and Joseph the Prophet was the
Lord's choice.

With an able scribe by his side, hour after
hour he added into biblical text what
earlier scribal tampering had removed.

During his months at the Johnson farmhouse Joseph was asked several times to interrupt the translation process to resolve pressing Church matters. Some matters were important, like proclaiming the gospel. "His mind, like Enoch's, expands as eternity, and God alone can comprehend his soul," one convert declared of his preaching.[21]

"hands . . . in my hair, and some had hold of my shirt, drawers and limbs," said Joseph. He struggled to free himself from their grasp but was threatened with death if he continued his resistance. The men swore "they would kill me if I did not be still, which quieted me."[24]

Joseph was carried by the men from the farmhouse

Joseph's caring for sick babies deeply touched me. I wanted to capture on canvas the love Joseph had for his children and the responsibility he felt for them and Emma. I found that loving image in this quiet moment when he walked the floor while Emma slept. ❧ ❧ ❧ ❧

Other matters were more trivial in nature, but any matter involving a child was carefully dealt with by Joseph: "I attended a special conference, to settle a difficulty which had occurred in Kirtland, on account of William Cahoon and Peter Devolue, having abused one of Brother Whitney's children."[22]

Attending to Church matters, preaching, and translating were the continuum of his labors in Hiram. However, on March 24, 1832, violence erupted in the community and Joseph's labors ended for a time. That evening, he and Emma were taking turns caring for their twins, who were seriously ill with measles.

As the evening wore on, Emma nursed the children while Joseph rested. Her scream of "Murder!" awakened him. He was startled to see a dozen violent-looking men, "disguised with colored faces and stimulated by whiskey," in the bedroom.[23] Some had their

to a sequestered area nearby. "You will have mercy and spare my life, I hope," he cried. Harsh profanities and laughter were followed by the directive, "Call on yer God for help, we'll show ye no mercy." They proceeded to "beat and scratch me well, tear off my shirt and drawers, and leave me naked," reported Joseph.[25] A mobber named Dr. Dennison tried to force an obnoxious drug into Josph's mouth but refused the urging of mobbers to emasculate him. However, the mobbers couldn't be quelled in their determination to tar and feather the Mormon prophet. The tar was fetched, and a mobber forced the tar paddle into Joseph's mouth, which all but smothered him. They covered his beaten body with tar, which rendered him unconscious. They next feathered him, and then fled in every direction.

As consciousness returned, Joseph struggled to rid the tar from his mouth to breathe more freely. He

While Emma Sleeps

The prospects of seeing a tomorrow grew dim for Joseph

as grown men reveled in violence.

I cannot hold back tears as I remember with sorrow

the night Joseph was tarred and feathered.

Three years have passed since our photo shoot

in which actors portrayed this violent

incident, and still I cannot paint it.

It is difficult to step

into this work and feel

Joseph's fear and

portray it on canvas. My

love and understanding

of the Prophet have grown

so much since the beginning of this project that what

I thought would be a matter-of-fact painting has proven

to be the most difficult of all. Simply, it is hard to see

such violence let loose on a prophet of God.

attempted to rise but failed. His second attempt was successful, and he slowly approached the Johnson farmhouse. Seeing Emma on the porch, he called to her. She could see that her husband was covered with something and assumed it was blood. She fainted. Joseph asked neighbors who were ministering to Emma if he could have a blanket, and a covering was found. Wrapping it around himself, he staggered into the farmhouse. Throughout the night his friends scraped and washed the tar from his wounded body.

Joseph survived the tarring and feathering ordeal, much to the chagrin of the mobbers. They were not appeased that he was "all scarified and defaced" by their cruelty.[26] Nor were they satisfied by the death of Joseph's infant son, who died a few days after the mobbing. (He was the fourth child of Joseph and Emma to succumb.) They wanted nothing less than the death of the Mormon Prophet.

Another pair of tiny hands

To lay beneath the clay

Slumb'ring little baby eyes

To wake another day

O God of heav'n

Come guard this bed

And let this angel sleep

Till earth is pure for tiny hands

And safe for tiny feet.[27]

Knowing the animosity of the mob element in Hiram, Joseph fled from the community. "God is my friend[;] in him I shall find comfort," he wrote to his wife. "I have given my life into his hands. . . . I Count not my life dear to me[,] only to do his will."[28]

Notes

1. Parley P. Pratt, ed., *Autobiography of Parley Parker Pratt* (Salt Lake City: Deseret Book Co., 1980), p. 48.

2. *HC* 1:146.

3. D&C 37:1; see also D&C 38.

4. "Newel Knight's Journal," *Scraps of Biography,* Faith-Promoting Series (Salt Lake City: Juvenile Instructor Office, 1883), 10:68.

5. *Painesville Telegraph,* 17 May 1831, p. 3, as cited in Porter, "New York Dissertation," p. 321.

6. *History of Geauga and Lake Counties, Ohio,* p. 248, as cited in Milton V. Backman Jr., *The Heavens Resound: A History of the Latter-day Saints in Ohio 1830–1838* (Salt Lake City: Deseret Book Co., 1983), p. 47.

7. *HC* 1:146n.

8. Remarks by Mary E. Lightner, Brigham Young University, 14 April 1905, p. 1; copy in BYU Archives, Harold B. Lee Library, Brigham Young University, Provo, Utah.

n.p., 1968), p. 17.

14. *HC* 1:215–16n.

15. *HC* 1:215.

16. Ibid.

17. *HC* 1:219.

18. *HC* 1:245.

19. *HC* 6:50.

20. D&C 76:22–23.

21. Wilford Woodruff in Journal History, as quoted by Preston Nibley, *Presidents of the Church* (Salt Lake City: Deseret Book Co., 1941), p. 139.

22. *HC* 1:219.

23. *Geauga Gazette,* 17 April 1832, as cited in Max H. Parkin, *Conflict at Kirtland: A Study of the Nature and Causes of External and Internal Conflict of the Mormons in Ohio between 1830 and 1838* (Salt Lake City: Max Parkin, 1967), p. 201.

24. *HC* 1:261.

25. *HC* 1:262–63.

As a mother I have wondered how I could face losing a child. Yet Emma lost six children. In focusing on the grief Emma experienced, I remember that Joseph grieved also. He lost six children too. This painting depicts their parental sorrow at the death of Joseph Murdock Smith. This infant would not be the last child Joseph and Emma would place beneath the clay.

9. Brigham Young, in *JD* 4:54.

10. *Painesville Telegraph,* 22 March 1831, p. 2.

11. *HC* 1:158.

12. George A. Smith, in *JD* 7:112.

13. Elden Jay Watson, *Manuscript History of Brigham Young, 1801–1844* (Salt Lake City:

26. *HC* 1:264.

27. Kenneth Cope, *My Servant Joseph* (Midvale, Utah: Embryo Music, 1993).

28. Jessee, *Personal Writings of Joseph Smith,* p. 239.

Tiny Hands

CHAPTER SIX

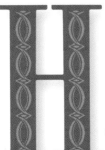

HOPING to escape the persecution of mobs, Joseph fled to the arms of his friends who were living in the frontier of Independence, Missouri. He arrived in Independence, or what the Lord called "the place for the city of Zion" or the New Jerusalem, on April 24, 1832, one month to the day after being tarred and feathered.[1] The Missouri Saints loved the Prophet and were overjoyed to have him with them. Joseph returned their love and wrote that his reception in Missouri was "a welcome only known by brethren and sisters united as one in the same faith, and by the same baptism, and supported by the same Lord."[2]

The change of scenery from Ohio to Missouri, however, had not dramatically changed the circumstances. An angry spirit of prejudice and hatred had mushroomed over the growth of Mormonism in Missouri. Joseph noted that the Saints "were settling among a ferocious set of mobbers, like lambs among wolves."[3] The Missourians found Mormonism a strange and threatening religion and sought

house of God"—a temple in Kirtland, Ohio.[4] When Joseph shared the revelation with the Ohio Saints, some suggested that the temple be a wood-framed building. Others requested the temple be constructed of logs.

"Shall we, brethren, build a house for our God, of logs?" Joseph asked. "No," he replied, "I have a better plan than that. I have a plan of the house of the Lord, given by himself."[5] The plan was intricate in detail and magnificent in design, but it was financially beyond the reach of the poverty-stricken Saints. "Notwithstanding

It didn't seem to matter whether Joseph was giving a sermon, playing ball, or working in his field. Where Joseph was, that is where his friends wanted to be. They saw in him a prophet who was young, strong, and athletic, who at one moment could enjoy cutting a log and at another share mysteries of God. I like to think that if I had known Joseph, I would have been among his friends.

occasions to ridicule and intimidate Saints living nearby. Disturbed by the unrelenting harassment upon his friends, Joseph counseled them to rise above retaliation and resolve to build New Jerusalem despite outward challenges. Encouraged by his words and with resolute determination, his followers clutched hammers, shovels, and spades and began anew to build the prophesied community.

After a few weeks Joseph bid farewell to his friends in Missouri and returned to Ohio. There the Lord revealed to him the importance of building "a house, even a house of prayer, a house of fasting, a house of faith, a house of learning, a house of glory, a house of order, a

the Church was poor," Joseph observed, and that "there was not a scraper and hardly a plow that could be found among the Saints," the followers of the Mormon prophet began to build the imposing edifice, and "our unity, harmony and charity abounded to strengthen us."[6]

Work on the temple commenced on June 5, 1833, when "George A. Smith hauled the first load of stone" and Hyrum Smith declared, "[I will] strike the first blow upon the house."[7] By summer 1833 nearly every able-bodied Saint had contributed time and labor to the construction of the temple.

Joseph, acting as the foreman in the stone quarry,

Strength of Body and Mind

said, "Come, brethren, let us go into the stone-quarry and work for the Lord."[8] Men left their fields unplanted and their shops unattended to answer his call. From cutting stones to felling trees, to milling, and to skilled carpentry, they worked night and day at a hurried pace to construct a temple that would glorify God. "Great exertions were made to expedite the work of the Lord's house," wrote Joseph.[9]

The women of the Church were as committed to building the house of the Lord as the men were. "Our wives were all the time knitting, spinning and sewing, and, in fact, I may say doing all kinds of work!" said Heber C. Kimball of the female contribution to the temple. "They were just as busy as any of us," he added.[10] "There was but one mainspring to all our thoughts and actions, and that was, the building of the Lord's house," declared Lucy Smith.[11]

Those with means to help construct the temple were as much needed as those with specific skills. "If ever God sent a man he sent you," remarked Joseph upon meeting newly baptized Thomas Grover. Grover had just arrived in Kirtland with five hundred dollars in his pocket, proceeds he had earned from selling his farm. "I want every dollar . . . that you have got in the world," said Joseph to Grover. The money was freely given.[12]

The joy of the Saints over the rising temple walls was countered by a growing mob element in Kirtland. Although friends readily defended Joseph, Mormonism, and the building of the temple, it seemed that each new stone added to the temple wall stirred the agitation of near neighbors to new heights. By winter of 1833–1834, mobs in Kirtland threatened to tear down the wall and kill the Mormon prophet. "Our enemies were raging and

threatening destruction upon us," Heber C. Kimball said. "We had to guard night after night, and . . . were obliged to lie with our fire-locks in our arms, to preserve Brother Joseph's life."[13] For weeks men did not remove their work clothes and "gave no sleep to their eyes, nor slumber to their eyelids" to protect the temple wall and the life of the Prophet.[14] Notwithstanding the threats of the mob, temple construction went steadily forward.[15]

Such could not be said of the Zion community in Independence, Missouri. Mob violence was not kept at bay in the frontier settlement, a town whose very name heralds man's inalienable rights. As flames of hatred erupted in Independence, Latter-day Saints were coated with tar and feathers. Among the victims was Edward Partridge, who wrote, "I bore my abuse with so much resignation and meekness, that it appeared to astound the multitude, who permitted me to retire in silence, many looking very solemn, their sympathies having been touched."[16]

The same meekness observed in Partridge went unnoticed in other Saints, who were also victimized by mobs. "All my property was scattered to the four winds, tools and all for pretended claims, where I owed not one cent justly," wrote Levi Hancock.[17] Joseph Knight attempted to preserve his property from pillage and destruction. "[I] submitted to the numerous indignities heaped upon [me], . . . [and] made many concessions to the mob in the hope of pacifying them, but it was useless."[18] Isaac Morley wrote in graphic detail of his struggles: "We were threatened day and night. They told us they would burn our house down over our heads. . . . The mob gave us no peace and all the while telling us we had to leave the country or they would kill us."[19]

By November 1833 persecuted Mormons in Missouri fled from unrestrained mobs across the Missouri River to Clay County. Without adequate shelter and food, many of the outcasts became ill. Others were more fortunate. However, "the condition of the scattered Saints is lamentable, and affords a gloomy prospect," wrote William W. Phelps to Joseph.[20]

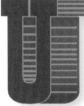PON RECEIVING word of the distressing circumstances of the Missouri Saints, Joseph "was overwhelmed with grief. He burst into tears and sobbed aloud, 'Oh my brethren! my brethren; . . . would that I had been with you, to have shared your fate. Oh my God, what shall I do in such a trial as this!'"[21] He wrote to his friends on the banks of the Missouri River, "When we learn of your sufferings, it awakens every sympathy of our hearts; it weighs us down; we cannot refrain from tears, yet, we are not able to realize, only in part, your sufferings."[22]

In answer to the Prophet's pleas to learn why such tribulations should befall his beloved Saints, Joseph learned, "I, the Lord, have suffered the affliction to come upon them, wherewith they have been afflicted, in consequence of their transgressions. . . . Therefore, they must needs be chastened and tried, even as Abraham."[23] Hoping to relieve the Abrahamic test of the Missouri Saints, Joseph made plans to come to their rescue. He "called a council [in Kirtland], and it was resolved, that the brethren from the surrounding country . . . should go immediately to Missouri, and take with them money and clothing to relieve the brethren in their distress."[24] He rallied the strength of the Ohio Saints to form a quasi-military force, the Army of the Lord, called Zion's Camp.

As the camp moved from Ohio to Missouri, Joseph counseled the men to keep the commandments of God and be united in faith, promising deliverance from their enemies, conditional upon their obedience. If unfaithful, the men were warned that the Lord "would visit them in his wrath" as he had the children of Israel and "vex them in his sore displeasure."[25]

Regarding the early days of the march toward Missouri, Joseph wrote, "God was with us. His angels went before us, and the faith of our little band was unwavering."[26] Yet, as the days on the march extended to weeks, failure to heed the divine warning evoked the wrath of God. An attack of infectious cholera erupted in the camp and spread quickly from man to man. "The brethren were so violently attacked that it seemed impossible to render them any assistance," said Joseph. "It seemed as though the heavens were sealed against us, and that every power that could render us any assistance was shut within its gates."[27]

Sixty-eight men were ill with cholera and thirteen died from it. As the Prophet tried to halt the spreading plague, he "learned by painful experience, that when the great Jehovah decrees destruction upon any people, and makes known His determination, man must not attempt to stay His hand."[28] The plague of illness and subsequent dispersion of Zion's Camp offered little promise to the exiled Saints living on the bluffs in the Missouri River Valley. To help them enjoy a union of believers Joseph organized the high council of Clay County on July 3, 1834, and set in order the affairs of the Church before again returning to Ohio.

In Ohio the Mormon prophet, who had "walked most of the [way to Missouri] and had a full proportion of blistered, bloody, and sore feet," was charged "with a catalogue of charges as black as the author of lies himself" for unbecoming conduct in Zion's Camp. Cries of "Tyrant—Pope—King—Usurper—Abuser" were shouted in a spirit of contention and apostasy.[29] Acquitted of wrongdoing in the camp, Joseph forgave his accusers and went about his work on the temple, but Mormon apostates were not appeased at the acquittal and aligned themselves with the mob element in Kirtland.

The growing contention did not divert the Prophet's concern for the Saints in Missouri or his desire to move temple construction forward. Money, produce, and letters of encouragement were sent to comfort Mormon exiles in their extremities. The loving gifts were well-received, and for a season the followers of Joseph in Missouri enjoyed a modicum of peace. During the same season Joseph and his friends in Kirtland finished the Kirtland Temple, and "there was much rejoicing in the Church, and great blessings were poured out upon the elders."[30] In the dedicatory prayer offered at the Kirtland Temple on March 27, 1836, the Prophet Joseph petitioned the Lord, "And we ask thee, Holy Father, that thy servants may go forth from this house armed with thy power, and that thy name may be upon them, and thy glory be round about them. . . . [Wilt thou] enable thy servants to seal up the law, and bind up the testimony."[31]

Convert Benjamin Brown heard the dedicatory prayer and testified to the fulfillment of Joseph's petition: "The Spirit of the Lord, as on the day of Pentecost, was profusely poured out. Hundreds of Elders spoke in tongues. . . . We had a most glorious and never-to-be-

I think the Lord had confidence in Emma that she could accomplish much good. Emma was given a musical talent and also the opportunity to be a comfort to Joseph and a mother to their children. How did she manage to accomplish all that was asked of her? How can I? I believe the answer lies in humble prayer and a desire to accomplish a righteous endeavor.

forgotten time. Angels were seen by numbers present."[32] Zebedee Coltrin further testified, "In the Kirtland Temple I have seen the power of God as it was on the day of Pentecost, and cloven tongues of fire have rested on the brethren, and they have spoken in other tongues as the Spirit gave them utterance. I saw the Lord high and lifted up. The angels of God rested upon the Temple and we heard their voices singing heavenly music."[33] The congregation sang these words with fervor:

> *The Spirit of God like a fire is burning!*
> *The latter-day glory begins to come forth;*
> *The visions and blessings of old are returning,*
> *And angels are coming to visit the earth.*[34]

Emma's Hymn

The heavens were opened, visions were seen, and the Saints shouted, "Hosannah to God and the Lamb." They then sealed their shout with a united "Amen!"[35]

Following this glorious day of dedication, newly baptized Prescindia Huntington recorded, "There was poured out upon us abundantly the spirit of revelation, prophe[c]y and tongues. The Holy Ghost filled the house; and along in the afternoon a noise was heard. It was the sound of a mighty rushing wind. . . . A little girl came to my door and in wonder called me out, exclaiming, 'The meeting is on the top of the meeting house!' I went to the door, and there I saw on the temple angels clothed in white covering the roof from end to end. They seemed to be walking to and fro; they appeared and disappeared. The third time they appeared and disappeared before I realized that they were not mortal men. Each time in a moment they vanished, and their reappearance was the same. This was in broad daylight, in the afternoon. A number of the children in Kirtland saw the same."[36]

One week after the dedication the Prophet Joseph wrote of another glorious manifestation in the temple. On the afternoon of April 3, 1836, "I retired to the pulpit, the veils being dropped, and bowed myself, with Oliver Cowdery, in solemn and silent prayer."[37] While praying, "the veil was taken from our minds, and the eyes of our understanding were opened. We saw the Lord standing upon the breastwork of the pulpit, before us; and under his feet was a paved work of pure gold, in color like amber."[38]

"His eyes were as a flame of fire; the hair of his head was white like the pure snow; his countenance shone above the brightness of the sun; and his voice was as the sound of the rushing of great waters, even the voice of Jehovah."[39] Joseph and Oliver heard the Savior say, "I have accepted this house. . . . And the fame of this house shall spread to foreign lands; and this is the beginning of the blessing which shall be poured out upon the heads of my people."[40]

The glory of that April day was never forgotten nor obscured by the serious difficulties that followed in 1837. In that year "it seemed as though all the powers of earth and hell were combining their influence in an especial manner to overthrow the Church at once, and make a final end," lamented the Prophet Joseph.[41] The self-appointed "reformers," including Warren Parrish, Stephen Burnett, and Sylvester Smith, publicly "rejected the Prophet, and denounced those who adhered to him as heretics."[42] The division created within Mormonism by apostates proved advantageous to anti-Mormons, whose "fruitful imaginations were aroused to the utmost, to invent new schemes to accomplish our destruction."[43]

The persecution gainst Joseph became so violent that he "regarded it as unsafe to remain any longer in Kirtland, and began to make arrangements to move to Missouri."[44] Faithful Saints followed his example. "What the Lord will do with us I know not," wrote the Prophet's uncle, John Smith, "altho he slay me I will trust in him. We are like the ancients wandering from place to place in the wilderness."[45]

At the very time the glory of Kirtland was reeling with apostasy, Mormonism in Missouri was following the same forbidden path. Disaffected Mormons from Kirtland had journeyed eight hundred miles "and contaminated the minds of many of the brethren [in Missouri]

Can you imagine a more glorious event than the
appearance of the Lord Jesus Christ in the Kirtland Temple?
Can you picture the joy of the builders in
knowing the temple was accepted
as a house of the Lord—
a holy sanctuary?
With the ancients of
Israel, I exclaim
"Hosanna" when I
remember that sacred day
in Kirtland, Ohio.

against Joseph, in order to destroy his influence."[47] Unfortunately, they found receptive listeners.

When the Prophet and Sidney Rigdon arrived in Missouri after hiding themselves in wagons "to elude the grasp of our pursuers who . . . [were] armed with pistols and guns, seeking our lives," they were greeted with mixed emotions.[47] The faithful expressed joy, as recorded by Joseph: "On the 14th of March, as we were about entering Far West, many of the brethren came out to meet us, who also with open arms welcomed us to their bosoms."[48] The disillusioned remained aloof but secretly

The atrocities against the followers of Joseph Smith are unparalleled on United States soil.

whispered innuendos that disclosed their contempt.

Among the disaffected was Oliver Cowdery, who said, "*Give me my freedom or take my life!* I shall no longer be bound by the chains of hell. I shall speak out when I see a move to deceive the ignorant."[49] David Whitmer falsely claimed that Joseph had led the Saints to "abandon the primitive faith" and "drift into error and spiritual blindness."[50] As slanderous hearsay spread, then escalated, attempts to establish truth were summarily dismissed as falsehoods. Solomon Hancock's unwavering testimony, "Brother Joseph is not a fallen prophet,

but will yet be exalted and become very high," went almost unnoticed amid vexatious lawsuits, name-calling, and betrayal of the Mormon prophet.[51]

As apostates joined their cry of "fallen prophet" with the mobocratic view of Joseph as a fanatic traitor, letters to Missouri civil leaders "begging their assistance against the 'Mormons'" proliferated. One letter "stated that Joseph Smith had, himself, killed seven men, . . . and that the inhabitants had every reason to expect that he would collect his people together, as soon as possible, and murder all that did not belong to his Church."[52] Believing the written falsehoods to be true and the escalating rumors to be valid, the governor of Missouri, Lilburn W. Boggs, called to arms the Missouri militia with orders to exterminate the Mormons or drive them from the state.

The Haun's Mill massacre and the fall of Adam-ondi-Ahman were outgrowths of the government sanctioned order to exterminate the Mormons. Frightened Latter-day Saints were subjected to the glitter of steel and the sheen of muskets as town after town fell to the Missouri militia. Hyrum Smith "endeavored to find out for what cause" the Mormons were being subjected to death. "All we could learn was, that it was because we were 'Mormons.'"[54]

The atrocities against the followers of Joseph Smith are unparalleled on United States soil. Convert Samuel Bent was tied to a tree and whipped by a mob. In reaction to the violence, it was recorded "that his faith is as ever and that he feels to praise God in prisons and in dungeons and in all circumstances whatever he may be found."[54] Simeon Carter was wounded in battle and "still determined to persevere and act in righteousness in all things, so that he might at last gain a crown of glory."[55] David Fullmer "had a severe sickness and was reduced nigh unto death. Before he recovered, the mob came and ordered us to leave our homes and go away in twenty-four hours or they would come and burn our homes and destroy our property."[56] William Huntington wrote, "I slept in my clothes with my rifle in my arms nearly one Month. . . . Our case now became alarming. It appeared the inhabitants Were determined to strip us of All means of getting out of the State."[57]

The exiled Saints who could escape the terror of extermination fled across the Mississippi River to spare their lives. Titus Billings' escape was plagued with starvation and frostbite, yet he wrote, "[I] never have had a writ served upon me not broken the law in one instance and now I say that these things have come upon us on account of the religion which we profess."[58] The tragedy endured by Billings was repeated again and again as thousands of Latter-day Saints sought refuge.

Notes

1. D&C 57:2.

2. HC 1:269.

3. Ibid.

4. D&C 88:119.

5. Smith, *History of Joseph Smith*, p. 230.

6. HC 1:349; Benjamin Johnson, "My Life's Review," pp. 10–11, as cited in Backman, *Heavens Resound*, p. 143.

7. HC 1:353; Smith, *History of Joseph Smith*, p. 231.

8. In JD 10:165.

9. HC 2:167.

10. Kimball, in JD 10:165.

11. Smith, *History of Joseph Smith*, p. 231.

12. Hetty M. P. Smith, "The Life of Thomas Grover, Utah Pioneer," p. 9.

13. Orson F. Whitney, *Life of Heber C. Kimball, an Apostle; the Father and Founder of the British Mission* (Salt Lake City: Juvenile Instructor Office, 1888), p. 46.

14. Smith, *History of Joseph Smith*, p. 231.

15. Ibid., p. 239.

16. HC 1:391.

17. Autobiography of Levi Ward Hancock, typescript, BYU Special Collections, p. 50.

18. Newel Knight, "Newel Knight's Journal," *Classic Experiences and Adventures* (Salt Lake City: Bookcraft, 1969), p. 97.

19. John Clifton Moffit, "Isaac Morley on the American Frontier," n.p., n.d., p. 9, in author's possession.

20. HC 1:457.

21. Smith, *History of Joseph Smith*, p. 225.

22. HC 1:454.

23. D&C 101:2, 4.

24. Smith, *History of Joseph Smith*, p. 225.

25. "Sketch of the Auto-biography of George Albert Smith," *Millennial Star* 27 (15 July 1865): 439.

26. HC 2:73.

27. Smith, *History of Joseph Smith*, pp. 228–29.

28. HC 2:114.

29. Journal of George A. Smith, 25 June 1834; HC 2:144.

30. Smith, *History of Joseph Smith*, p. 239.

31. D&C 109:22, 46.

32. Benjamin Brown, *Testimonies for the Truth* (Liverpool: S. W. Richards, 1853), pp. 10–11.

33. Minutes of the Salt Lake City School of the Prophets, October 10–11, 1883, as cited in Andrus, *They Knew the Prophet*, p. 29.

34. *Hymns of The Church of Jesus Christ of Latter-day Saints* (Salt Lake City: The Church of Jesus Christ of Latter-day Saints, 1985), no. 2.

35. HC 2:427–28.

36. Edward W. Tullidge, *The Women of Mormondom* (New York: n.p., 1877), pp. 209, 208.

37. D&C 110, Introduction.

38. D&C 110:1–2.

39. D&C 110:3.

40. D&C 110:7, 10.

41. HC 2:487.

42. B. H. Roberts, *A Comprehensive History of The Church of Jesus Christ of Latter-day Saints*, 6 vols. (Provo, Utah: Brigham Young University Press, 1965), 1:405.

43. Smith, *History of Joseph Smith*, p. 247.

44. Ibid.

45. Journal of John Smith, 23 April 1838.

46. Smith, *History of Joseph Smith*, p. 243.

47. HC 3:2–3.

48. HC 3:8–9.

49. Huntington Library Letters, microfilm no. 87, as cited in Stanley R. Gunn, *Oliver Cowdery, Second Elder and Scribe* (Salt Lake City: Bookcraft, 1962), p. 230.

50. David Whitmer, *An Address to All Believers in Christ* (Richmond, Missouri: n.p., 1887).

51. HC 3:225.

52. Smith, *History of Joseph Smith*, p. 254.

53. HC 3:420.

54. Donald Q. Cannon and Lyndon W. Cook, eds., *Far West Record: Minutes of The Church of Jesus Christ of Latter-day Saints, 1830–1844* (Salt Lake City: Deseret Book Co., 1983), p. 222.

55. HC 3:225.

56. "Experiences in the Life of Rhoda Ann Fullmer," n.p., n.d., p. 2, in author's possession.

57. Journal of William Huntington, pp. 4, 8, in author's possession.

58. Clark V. Johnson, ed., *Mormon Redress Petitions: Documents of the 1833–1838 Missouri Conflict* (Provo, Utah: Religious Studies Center, Brigham Young University, 1992), pp. 139–40.

CHAPTER SEVEN

OSEPH Smith and

other Mormon leaders did not escape the extremities of

Missouri. "We had no confidence in the word" of the militia

leaders camped outside the Mormon settlement of Far West,

wrote Parley P. Pratt. However, seeing "no alternative but to put ourselves

into the hands of such monsters, or to have the city attacked, and men, women and

children massacred," Joseph, his brother Hyrum, Sidney Rigdon, Parley Pratt, and a few others "commended [them]selves to the Lord, and voluntarily surrendered as sheep into the hands of wolves."[1]

As word spread through the militia camp of the capture of Joseph Smith, men began yelling "like so many bloodhounds let loose upon their prey," wrote Pratt. "If the vision of the infernal regions could suddenly open to the mind, with thousands of malicious fiends, all clamoring . . . raging and foaming like a troubled sea, then could some idea be formed of the hell which we had entered."[2]

The parents of the Prophet also listened to the harrowing sounds that punctuated the air of Far West that night. Mother Smith reported that "had the army been composed of so many bloodhounds, wolves, and panthers, they could not have made a sound more terrible. . . . [We] could distinctly hear their horrid yellings. Not knowing the cause, we supposed they were murdering [Joseph]." When guns discharged, Father Smith cried, "Oh, my God! my God! they have killed my son! they have murdered him! and I must die, for I cannot live without him!" With her own "unutterable agony," Mother Smith "assisted [her husband] to the bed and he fell back upon it helpless as a child."[3]

Throughout the evening hours the guards "kept up a constant tirade of mockery, and the most obscene blackguardism and abuse. They blasphemed God; mocked Jesus Christ; swore the most dreadful oaths;

taunted brother Joseph and others; demanded miracles; wanted signs, such as: 'Come, Mr. Smith, show us an angel.' 'Give us one of your revelations.' 'Show us a miracle.' . . . 'Or, if you are Apostles or men of God, deliver yourselves, and then we will be Mormons.'"[4]

On November 1, 1838, a court-martial was held to determine the fate of Joseph and his fellow captives. Fourteen officers, twenty preachers, and a few local judges were present. When the court ended near midnight, General Lucas issued an order to General

I like Lucy. When others quailed at the sight of the Missouri militia, she boldly pressed through the crowd to speak to her son. Prison wagon or not, she was not diverted. Perhaps it is from Lucy that Joseph learned the value of persistence. In this painting I hope to convey my admiration of Lucy Mack Smith, a mother who knew joys and sorrows.

Alexander Doniphan to execute the prisoners: "Sir:—You will take Joseph Smith and the other prisoners into the public square of Far West, and shoot them at 9 o'clock tomorrow morning." Doniphan refused to comply: "It is cold blooded murder. I will not obey your order. . . . If you execute these men, I will hold you responsible before an earthly tribunal, so help me God."[5]

Doniphan's defiance, and that of a few others, "so alarmed the haughty murderer and his accomplices that

God Bless You, Mother!

they dare not put the decree in execution."[6] Rather than free the prisoners, they forced them to climb inside wagons which would convey them to Independence. A request by the prisoners to bid their families farewell and obtain a change of clothing was reluctantly granted.

A guard of six men accompanied Joseph to his home at Far West. There he found his wife and children in tears, fearing that he had been shot. A moment of privacy to comfort them was denied by guards who brandished swords. When Joseph's six-year-old son asked, "Father, is the mob going to kill you?" a guard pushed the boy aside and said, "You d— little brat, go back; you will see your father no more."[7]

Joseph was shoved back into the prisoners' wagon. Multitudes gathered to see him one last time but were prevented by the strong cloth covering that was nailed atop the wagon. Among the throng that gathered was his mother. "I am the mother of the Prophet—is there not a gentleman here, who will assist me to that wagon, that I may take a last look at my children, and speak to them once more before I die?" she exclaimed.[8] A pathway was

I profess to be nothing but a man, and a minister of salvation, sent by Jesus Christ to preach the Gospel.

made and she was taken to the back of one of the wagons.

"Mr. Smith, your mother and sister are here, and wish to shake hands with you," a man called out. As a hand was thrust through the cloth covering, Mother Smith cried, "Joseph, do speak to your poor mother once more—I cannot bear to go till I hear your voice." Amid sobs Joseph said, "God bless you, mother!"[9]

The wagons then slowly moved away from the city. A feeling of doom overcame the captives as they moved toward Independence until Joseph whispered, *Be of good cheer, brethren; the word of the Lord came to me last night that our lives should be given us, and that whatever we may suffer during this captivity, not one of our lives should be taken."*[10]

Many curiosity seekers clamored to see the Mormon leaders as the wagons neared Independence. "Which of the prisoners [is] the Lord whom the 'Mormons' worship?" a woman asked. When a soldier pointed to Joseph, she approached him and inquired "whether [he] professed to be the Lord and Savior?" Joseph replied, "I profess to be nothing but a man, and a minister of salvation, sent by Jesus Christ to preach the Gospel."[11] He then preached a discourse on the doctrines of faith, repentance, baptism, and the Holy Ghost. "All seemed surprised, and the lady, in tears, went her way, praising God for the truth, and praying aloud that the Lord would bless and deliver the prisoners."[12]

Instead of being delivered from captivity, the prisoners were taken to a vacant wooden house and placed under military guard. Surprising to Joseph, his friends, and the guards were the "hundreds [that] flocked to see us day after day. We spent most of our time in preaching and conversation, explanatory of our doctrines and practice. Much prejudice was removed, and the feelings of the populace began to be in our favor, notwithstanding their former wickedness and hatred."[13]

After a brief confinement in Independence, the prisoners were escorted by military guards to Richmond, Missouri. On November 10, 1838, they were confined in a ramshackle log cabin. Their legs were chained and padlocked by the state prison keeper, while guards kept guns pointed at them. Joseph described the chains that bound the prisoners: "Brother Robison is chained next to me he has a true heart and a firm mind, Brother Wight, is next,

Br. Rigdon, next, Hyrum, next, Parley, next Amasa, next, and thus we are bound together in chains as well as the cords of everlasting love, we are in good spirits and rejoice that we are counted worthy to be persecuted for Christ['s] sake."[14]

T hus . . . bound together in chains as well as the cords of everlasting love, we are in good spirits.

Common courtesies such as providing utensils for eating were denied the prisoners, who were forced to eat with their fingers. Joseph's distress from toothache and fever caused by exposure to cold weather was ignored. Due to illness Sidney Rigdon was delirious, but his fainting spells, fits of uncontrollable laughter, and incoherent speech were mocked. Adding to their trials was the profane cursing and taunting of the guards. "I had listened till I became so disgusted, shocked, horrified, and so filled with the spirit of indignant justice that I could scarcely refrain from rising upon my feet and rebuking the guards," wrote Pratt.[15] However, he was not the one to silence them.

"On a sudden [Joseph] arose to his feet, and spoke in a voice of thunder, or as the roaring lion . . . : '*SILENCE, ye fiends of the infernal pit. In the name of Jesus Christ I rebuke you, and command you to be still; I*

Majesty in Chains

I wanted to paint hate in Joseph's countenance to mirror my feelings for the militia guards in the Richmond jail. But I could not. I believe Joseph loved these men but felt great sorrow for the suffering they inflicted upon his friends. Perhaps as he listened to their boisterous boasts about atrocities, it was as if they were abusing his friends anew. With power and with majesty he rebuked them.

will not live another minute and hear such language. Cease such talk, or you or I die THIS INSTANT!'

" . . . He stood erect in terrible majesty. Chained, and without a weapon; calm, unruffled and dignified," wrote Pratt. There was such a tone of finality in Joseph's words, such an air of commanding authority in his bearing, that he silenced the "quailing guards, whose weapons

hostile audience, already convinced that the prisoners were guilty, intimidated the witnesses and defendants throughout the hearing. One member of the hostile crowd shouted, "There is a red hot Mormon, d-m him, I am acquainted with him." Others blurted out, "That dam rascal was in the battle—or out to Davis—or to DeWit, such a one is a great preacher and leader amongst them,

We have waded through practiced upon us by the

were lowered or dropped to the ground; whose knees smote together, and who, shrinking into a corner, or crouching at his feet, begged his pardon, and remained quiet till a change of guards."[16]

The civil hearing for the prisoners, often referred to as a mock trial, began on November 12, 1838. The Honorable Austin A. King, fifth judicial circuit court judge, presided. King gladly welcomed crowds of spectators who gathered in the unfurnished courthouse to observe the proceedings and taunt the defendants. The

he ought to be hung, or sent to the penitentiary." Judge King made no attempt to quell the outbursts. Even when one of the prison guards shouted, "Shoot your Mormon, I have shot mine," King remained unruffled.[17]

After the first day of the court proceedings, Governor Boggs received a letter assuring him of the guilt of the Mormon leaders: "We progress slowly, but thus far the disclosures indicate certain conviction of treason against Smith, Wight, Pratt, Rigdon, and some one or two more; and of murder against some five or six; burglary against several; arson against a number; and larceny against others. How it will all result, I cannot tell, but that the leaders will be convicted of treason or murder I think is certain and many others of felony."[18] On the same day, Joseph wrote to his wife Emma, "My Dear Emma, we are prisoners in chains, and under strong guards, for Christ['s] sake and for no other cause, . . . but on

perjured witnesses who sought to verify old rumors by creating new ones. "Renegade 'Mormon' dissenters are . . . spreading various foul and libelous reports against us, thinking thereby to gain the friendship of the world. . . . We have waded through an ocean of tribulation and mean abuse, practiced upon us by the ill bred and the ignorant," said Joseph.[20]

an ocean of tribulation and mean abuse ll bred and the ignorant.

examination, I think that the authorities, will discover our innocence, and set us free. . . . I am your husband and am in bands and tribulation &c—"[19]

The remaining fourteen days of the trial focused on alleged Mormon raiding expeditions in northern Missouri counties and the suspected treason of Mormon leaders. The prosecution called forty-one witnesses, twenty Missourians and twenty-one Mormons, who were sworn in at the point of a bayonet. Day after day the weary prisoners listened to a seemingly endless parade of

Judge King did not view the dissenting Mormons as renegades but as convincing witnesses. His prejudice against the Mormon leaders was apparent in his cross-examinations. For example, after eliciting testimony about Joseph's interpretation of Daniel 7:27, regarding the kingdom of God rolling forth and destroying all earthly kingdoms, Judge King instructed the clerk, *"Write that down; it is a strong point for treason."* The defense attorney served: "Judge, you had better make the Bible treason." King did not reply.[21]

Following the examination of the prosecution witnesses, the defense attempted to introduce witnesses on behalf of the prisoners. Forty or fifty names of defense witnesses were submitted to Judge King. He promptly turned the list over to a captain in the Missouri militia for further arrests. A second attempt resulted in the same charade. However, seven witnesses, four men and three women, evaded the threats and the intimidations of the court and testified in behalf of the prisoners, but to no avail. Following their testimonies, the prosecution called a final witness, who denied that the Missouri militia had threatened any Mormon settlers.

N THE BASIS of the evidence presented, Judge King found probable cause to order Joseph Smith, Hyrum Smith, Sidney Rigdon, Lyman Wight, Caleb Baldwin, and Alexander McRae to be jailed in Liberty, Clay County, Missouri, on charges of overt acts of treason.

Angered by the decision, the defense attorney exclaimed, "If a cohort of angels were to come down, and declare [the prisoners] innocent, it would all be the same; for [King] had determined from the beginning to cast [them] into prison."[22] The prisoners viewed the court as a farce, merely another abuse heaped upon them by enemies under the guise of the law. Joseph believed the hearing to be a "mock examination" in which "there was not the least shadow of honor, or justice, or law, administered toward them, but sheer prejudice, and the spirit of persecution and malice."[23]

The next day the six prisoners were chained, handcuffed, placed in a wagon, and taken to Liberty. On December 1 they were locked in the squalor of Liberty Jail. "Our place of lodging was the square side of hewed white oak logs, and our food was anything but good and decent," stated Joseph's brother Hyrum. "Poison was administered to us three or four times. . . . The poison would inevitably have proved fatal had not the power of Jehovah interposed in our behalf, to save us from their wicked purpose."[24] The prisoners petitioned the supreme court of Missouri twice for a writ of habeas corpus, but were denied. Unofficially, they were told "*there was no law for the Mormons in the State of Missouri.*"[25] Joseph concluded, "The soldiers and officers of every kind hated us, and the most profane blasphemers and drunkards & whoremongers hated us, they all hated us most cordially. And now what did they hate us for, purely because of the testimony of Jesus Christ."[26]

Although left without external hope and with enemies seeking their blood on every side, Joseph penned letters of encouragement to his wife and friends. Indeed it may be said that "the eyes of the saints were turned to [Liberty Jail] as the place whence would come encouragement, counsel—the word of the Lord. It was more temple than prison, so long as the Prophet was there."[27]

To Emma, Joseph wrote, "As to yourself if you want to know how much I want to see you, examine your feelings, how much you want to see me, and Judge for yourself, I would gladly walk from here to you barefoot, and bareheaded, and half naked, to see you and think it great pleasure, and never count it toil." Two weeks earlier he had written, "Dear Emma[,] I very well know your toils and simpathize with you if God will spare my life once more to have the privelege of takeing care of you I will ease your care and indeavour to cumfort your heart." In writing of his children he admonished his wife to "not let those little fellows . . . forgit me, tell them Father loves them with a perfect love, and he is doing all he can to git away from the mob to come to them."[28]

To his friends who had escaped from the terrors of the extermination order, the Mormon prophet wrote letters of counsel and direction, assuring them of the omnipotent power of the Lord to deliver his Saints from their extremities: "What power shall stay the heavens? As well might man stretch forth his puny arm to stop the Missouri river in its decreed course, or to turn it up stream, as to hinder the Almighty from pouring down knowledge from heaven upon the heads of the Latter-day Saints."[29]

When hope seemed only a momentary glimmer, Joseph cried, "O God, where art thou? And where is the pavilion that covereth thy hiding place? How long shall thy hand be stayed, and thine eye, yea thy pure eye, behold from the eternal heavens the wrongs of thy people and of thy servants, and thine ear be penetrated with their cries?[30]

The Lord comforted his imprisoned prophet, "My son, peace be unto thy soul; thine adversity and thine afflictions shall be but a small moment; And then, if thou endure it well, God shall exalt thee on high; thou shalt triumph over all thy foes. Thy friends do stand by thee, and they shall hail thee again with warm hearts and friendly hands. Thou are not yet as Job; thy friends do not contend against thee, neither charge thee with transgression,

as they did Job. . . . If the very jaws of hell shall gape open the mouth wide after thee, know thou, my son, that all these things shall give thee experience, and shall be for thy good. The Son of Man hath descended below them all. Art thou greater than he? . . . Fear not what man can do, for God shall be with you forever and ever."[31]

Notes

1. Pratt, *Autobiography of Parley P. Pratt,* p. 186.

2. Ibid., 187.

3. Smith, *History of Joseph Smith,* p. 289.

4. Pratt, *Autobiography of Parley P. Pratt,* p. 187.

5. Joseph Fielding Smith, *Essentials of Church History* (Salt Lake City: Deseret Book Co., 1953), p. 241.

6. Pratt, *Autobiography of Parley P. Pratt,* p. 188.

7. *HC* 3:447.

8. Smith, *History of Joseph Smith,* p. 290.

9. Ibid., pp. 290–91.

10. Pratt, *Autobiography of Parley P. Pratt,* p. 192.

11. *HC* 3:200–201.

12. Pratt, *Autobiography of Parley P. Pratt,* p. 193.

13. Ibid., p. 195.

14. Correspondence from Joseph Smith to Emma Smith, 12 November 1838, as cited in Jessee, *Personal Writings of Joseph Smith,* p. 368.

15. Pratt, *Autobiography of Parley P. Pratt,* pp. 210–11.

16. Ibid., p. 211.

17. E. Robinson, "Items of Person History," *The Return,* 2 (March 1890): 16, 234; as cited

in Stephen C. LeSueur, *The 1838 Mormon War in Missouri* (Columbia, Missouri: University of Missouri Press, 1987), p. 198.

18. Correspondence from John B. Clark to Lilburn W. Boggs, as cited in Leland Gentry, p. 544.

19. Correspondence from Joseph Smith to Emma Smith, 12 November 1838, as cited in Jessee, *Personal Writings of Joseph Smith,* pp. 367–68.

20. *HC* 3:231–32.

21. Pratt, *Autobiography of Parley P. Pratt,* p. 212.

22. *HC* 3:213.

23. Affidavit of Joseph Smith et al., 15 March 1839, as cited in Heman C. Smith, ed., "Appeals to Supreme Court of Missouri," *Journal of History* 9 (April 1916): 206.

24. Pratt, *Autobiography of Parley P. Pratt,* pp. 219–20.

25. Ibid., p. 222.

26. Jessee, *Personal Writings of Joseph Smith,* p. 377.

27. Roberts, *Comprehensive History,* 1:526.

28. Jessee, *Personal Writings of Joseph Smith,* pp. 426, 408.

29. D&C 121:33.

30. D&C 121:1–3.

31. D&C 121:7–10; 122:7–9.

CHAPTER EIGHT

JOSEPH'S followers forded the icy Mississippi River to seek refuge in Illinois from the atrocities caused by the extermination order. Witnessing their crossing of the might river was attorney O. H. Browning: "Great God! have I not seen it? Yes, my eyes have beheld the blood-stained traces of innocent women and children, in the drear winter, who had traveled hundreds of miles barefoot, through frost and snow, to seek a refuge from their savage pursuers."[1]

For exiled Mormons the Illinois bank of the Mississippi provided a place of safety from the hatred and bigotry they had known in Missouri. Although the Saints were grateful to be free from religious persecution, discouragement and frustration over the continued incarceration of Joseph permeated their thoughts. Freeing him from the loathsome Missouri jail seemed paramount to their happiness and was their prayer to God both night and day.

Freedom was granted to the Mormon prophet and fellow prisoners by a most unusual turn of events. On April 5, 1839, they were awarded a change of venue to Gallatin, Missouri, meaning the prisoners were to be transported to a new location, there to be tried for alleged crimes. Less than a week passed before, on April 11, 1839, Joseph and four others were granted another change of venue from Gallatin to Columbia in Boone County. As they journeyed with prison guards toward Boone County, the guards became intoxicated. "We thought it a favorable opportunity to make our escape," wrote Joseph.[2] Rather than the change prescribed by Missouri law, "We took our change of venue for the state of Illinois."[3]

Anticipating their arrival in Quincy, Illinois, was their mother, Lucy Smith. "After falling asleep," she recalled, "I saw my sons in vision. They were upon the prairie traveling, and seemed very tired and hungry." This dream awoke her and she, in turn, awoke her husband. "Oh, Mr. Smith, I can see Joseph and Hyrum, and they are so weak they can hardly stand. Now they are lying asleep on the cold ground! Oh, how I wish that I could give them something to eat!" Father Smith, "begged [her] to be quiet," but she refused his request and walked the

floor until morning, when she "made preparations to receive [her] sons, confident that the poor, afflicted wanderers would arrive at home before sunset."[4]

That afternoon Joseph and Hyrum crossed the Mississippi and arrived in Quincy. "They went immediately to see their families" and were lovingly embraced.[5] Their friends also greeted them with heartfelt warmth. "No man can understand the joyful sensations created . . . , except those who have been in tribulation for the Gospel's sake," wrote Wilford Woodruff upon greeting Joseph.[6] For Parley Pratt the meeting was filled with emotion: "Neither of us could refrain from tears as we embraced each other once more as free men. We felt like shouting hosannah in the highest, and giving glory to that God who had delivered us in fulfilment of His word." Joseph then blessed Pratt "with a warmth of sympathy and brotherly kindness which I shall never forget."[7]

The Prophet desired to bless all the suffering Saints by creating for them a refuge from the storms of persecution and hatred, a place to worship God, a city on a hill. Near an unlikely bluff overlooking a swampy bend in the Mississippi River the plans to build such a city unfolded in 1839. In that year speculators scurried to find buyers for investments gone sour in the swamplands of Illinois. They offered to sell the infested marshland called Commerce for almost no money down. The Mormon exiles could afford little more and so the purchase price of the swamp was agreed upon. In describing the purchase Joseph said, "The place was literally a wilderness. The land was mostly covered with trees and bushes, and much of it so wet that it was with the utmost difficulty a footman could get through, and totally impossible for teams." Yet with "no more eligible place presenting itself," the Mormon prophet "considered it wisdom to make an attempt to build up a city."[8] Following the advice of Joseph, his followers moved to Commerce and lived in makeshift tents and wagons as they worked to acquire the needed materials to build log cabins.

Many Saints became ill at this time, due to months of severe physical and emotional hardship. With outstretched arms Joseph and Emma welcomed the suffering Saints into their home in Commerce until it "became so crowded that they were compelled to spread a tent."[9] Wilford Woodruff recalled Joseph living in the tent: "It was a very sickly time; Joseph had given up his home in Commerce to the sick, and had a tent pitched in his dooryard and was living in that himself."[10]

Mother Smith also contracted the strange fever that infested the Saints living in marshy lowlands. "I was taken very sick and was brought nigh unto death," she recalled. "For five nights Emma never left me, but stood at my bedside all the night long, at the end of which time she was overcome with fatigue and taken sick herself. Joseph then took her place and watched with me the five succeeding nights, as faithfully as Emma had done."[11]

On the morning of July 22, 1839, the Prophet called upon the Lord in mighty prayer, asking for the gift to heal his loved ones. That gift was bestowed upon Joseph throughout the day. By the laying on of hands, he healed all in his household and those lying in tents in his yard. As he walked among the sick lying near the Mississippi River, he asked in the name of Jesus Christ that they be restored to health. His request was granted. He then crossed the river to the Iowa side to bless Mormons lying ill near the banks. Again he was blessed to heal the sick.

Wilford Woodruff recalled the Prophet coming to Elijah Fordham's bedside and asking, "Brother Fordham,

By the laying on of hands, he healed all in his household and those lying in tents in his yard.

do you not know me?" Elijah did not respond. Joseph asked again, "Elijah, do you not know me?" A faint whispered "yes" was heard. "Have you not faith to be healed?" Joseph asked. "I am afraid it is too late; if you had come sooner, I think I might have been," he said. The Prophet then queried, "Do you believe that Jesus is

answer from his father. "You shall even live to finish your work," his father promised him. Joseph cried out, "Oh! my father, shall I?" "Yes," said his father, "you shall live to lay out the plan of all the work which God has given you to do."[13]

Joseph, relieved by the patriarchal assurance, went forward with confidence. He set aside his rebuff from United States President Martin Van Buren (who said, "Your cause is just; but I can do nothing for you!") as a faint memory of yesteryear. Schemes of John C. Bennett and other enemies to destroy his influence became only shadows of past wrongs. For a brief season the people of Nauvoo and their Prophet saw that "sickness ceased from among us and the mob retired to their homes," and the fledgling city became a haven for the faithful and a curiosity to near neighbors and casual passersby.[14]

The sick left beds of affliction, and those with wavering faith were healed, both body and spirit, when Joseph walked near the Mississippi River that hot summer day. To have seen the miracle or to have been among the healed would have been an unspeakable joy. It is reminiscent of the days of old when Jesus of Nazareth caused the blind to see, the lame to walk, and the afflicted to rise. I am grateful the day of healing continues.

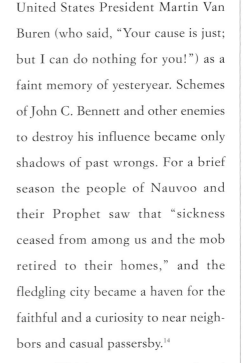

the Christ?" Meekly, he replied, "I do, Brother Joseph." In a commanding voice the Prophet said, "Elijah, I command you, in the name of Jesus of Nazareth, to arise and be made whole."[12] Fordham immediately arose from his bed, dressed, ate, and followed the Prophet into the street and watched as he blessed others.

After that miraculous day of healing, the strange disease did not subside but mercilessly attacked both young and old. With illness and death on every side, Joseph questioned whether he would also succumb. He sought the

With hammer, saw, trowel, and shovel, the Saints began to replace the squalor of makeshift tents and log cottages with permanent structures. Home and shop next to barn and stable, with a family garden in between, quickly became the norm. Joseph told settlers along the Mississippi that he "would build up a city, and the old inhabitants replied 'We will be damned if you can.' So I prophesied that I would build up a city, and the inhabitants prophesied that I could not."[15] The city became known as "The City Beautiful" and contrasted with the meandering river as its inhabitants built gristmills,

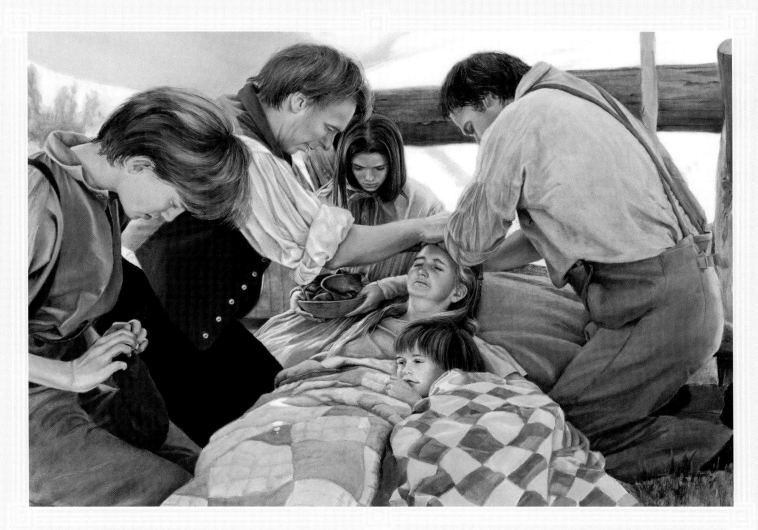

A Day of God's Power

lumber mills, potteries, tanneries, brickyards, bakeries, and dozens of other home industries that surprised the erstwhile observer. "Nauvoo grew, with magic rapidity, from a few rude homes to a magnificent city," wrote diarist Harvey Cluff. "Houses increased in number, farms were opened up and prairie lands east of the city con-

the critical visitor. "Sadly was I disappointed," wrote Reverend Samuel Prior after his visit to Nauvoo. "Instead of seeing a few miserable log cabins and mud hovels, which I had expected to find, I was surprised to see one of the most romantic places that I had visited in the West. The buildings, though many of them were small

 **hat unspeakable delight—and what transports of joy swelled my bosom—when I took by the hand, on that night, my beloved Emma—she that was my wife, even the wife of my youth, and the choice of my heart! Many were the vibrations of my mind when I contemplated for a moment the many scenes we had been called to pass through, the fatigues and the toils, the sorrows and suffering, and the joys and consolations. . . . Oh, what a commingling of thoughts filled my mind for the moment! And again she is here, even in the seventh trouble—undaunted, firm and unwavering—unchangeable, affectionate Emma!"[17]**

verted into prosperous fields of golden grain."[16] Tinsmith, baker, cobbler, and potter were all hard at work. "You could look over the little settlement and see the hand of industry in every corner of the town," wrote John Butler.[18]

J. H. Buckingham, a gentleman from Boston, penned, "No one can visit Nauvoo, and come away without a conviction that . . . the body of the Mormons were an industrious, hard-working, and frugal people. In the history of the whole world there cannot be found such another instance of so rapid a rise of a city out of the wilderness—a city so well built, a territory so well cultivated."[19]

The mere fact that the Mormons were succeeding on a swamp when contemporaries in advantageous eastern cities were destitute was unique, if not frustrating, to

and of wood, yet bore the marks of neatness which I have not seen equalled in this country."[20]

Of all the buildings constructed in Nauvoo, none was as magnificent as the Nauvoo Temple. "The Temple exceeds in splendor and magnificence any building I have ever seen," penned Jacob Scott.[21] "I am not capacitated to build according to the world," Joseph told the *Pittsburgh Gazette* editor. "I know nothing about architecture and all that."[22] Yet he had definite ideas about how the Nauvoo Temple should be constructed. To architect William Weeks he said, "I wish you to carry out my designs. I have seen in vision the splendid appearance of that building illuminated, and will have it built according to the pattern shown me."[23]

While Weeks struggled to draw his architectural

My Beloved Emma

Flowers for a Lady

renderings to the specifications seen in the vision, work in the limestone quarries began. Tons of stone were retrieved from the ravine and pushed and pulled to the temple site to be polished. Men hauled stone day after day by hitching teams up to wagons and pulling the stones through the streets, which were too often muddy. Joseph, seeing Brother Bybee's wagon stuck in a mud hole, "wad[ed] in mud halfway to his knees and [got] his shoulder covered with mud to help another man in distress."[24] He was not above the physical exertion of pushing and pulling a wagon, cutting limestone, or chopping wood. "I love to wait upon the Saints, and be a servant to all," he said.[25]

E WAS OFTEN INTERRUPTED in his physical labor when a friend requested, "Brother Joseph, talk to us." A gospel conversation would soon ensue. "I could lean back and listen. Ah what pleasure this gave me," wrote Wandle Mace. "[The Prophet] would unravel the scriptures and explain doctrine as no other man could. What had been mystery he made so plain it was no longer mystery."[26] Brigham Young added, "[Joseph] took heaven, figuratively speaking, and brought it down to earth; and he took the earth, brought it up, and opened up, in plainness and simplicity, the things of God."[27]

Acknowledged as a prophet by his followers and as the "town architect" by friend and foe alike, he was applauded for the industry, growth, and overall development of Nauvoo. Joseph wanted no plaudits or recognition, even though he was recognized as the Mayor of

When riding with him and his wife Emma in their carriage I have known him to alight and gather prairie flowers for my little girl.

Nauvoo and the Lieutenant General of the Nauvoo Legion. He only wished that he could do more for those who sacrificed family, friends, and homeland to build Nauvoo. One such individual, Jane Robinson, wrote, "It was a severe trial to me, in my feelings to leave my native land and the pleasing associations that I had formed there." But she also reaffirmed her choice in the following words: "My heart was fixed. I knew in whom I had trusted and with the fire of Israel's God burning in my bosom, I forsook my home."[28]

For these Saints, Joseph gave up necessities of life to better serve them. He wrote, "My house has been a home and resting-place for thousands, and my family many times obliged to do without food, after having fed all they had to visitors."[29] One Latter-day Saint suggested that to remedy the problem of feeding so many visitors

Joseph "must do as [Napoleon] Bonaparte did—have a little table, just large enough for the victuals you want yourself." Emma replied, "Mr. Smith is a bigger man than Bonaparte: he can never eat without his friends."[30]

The Prophet Joseph loved his wife Emma and was not above assisting her. "Emma began to be sick with fever; consequently I kept in the house with her all day," he wrote in his journal.[31] At a party held in their home, "twenty-one [guests] sat down to the dinner-table, and Emma and myself waited on them," wrote Joseph.[32] One Latter-day Saint, observing Joseph doing "woman's work" to relieve the burdens of his wife, concluded that misman-agement of home chores by Emma was the root of the domestic problems. "I said to him, 'Brother Joseph, my wife does much more hard work than does your wife.' [He] replied by telling me that if a man cannot learn in this life to appreciate a wife and do his duty by her, in properly taking care of her, he need not expect to be given one in the hereafter." The judgmental advisor wrote, "His words shut my mouth as tight as a clam. I took them as terrible reproof. After that I tried to do better by the good wife I had and tried to lighten her labors."[33]

Joseph's tenderness towards his wife was characteristic of his kindness to others. When he learned that a member of the Church had lost his home from a raging fire, he reached into his pocket and pulled out a five-dollar coin and said, "I feel sorry for this brother to the amount of five dollars; how much do you feel sorry?"[34] The widow of Robert Thompson wrote of Joseph's kindness after the death of her husband, "This indeed was a time of sorrow, but I can never forget the tender sympathy and brotherly kindness [Joseph] ever showed toward me and my fatherless child. When riding with him and his wife Emma in their carriage I have known him to alight and gather prairie flowers for my little girl."[35]

Such was the caring nature of the Mormon prophet. His concern for "the one" led him to hope that Nauvoo had become a refuge for the Saints of God and the storms of the past were only faint memories. He and his followers enjoyed a brief repose from their struggles, and it seemed for a season that all was well.

But the seeds of Joseph's demise had already been planted among his followers and could not be uprooted. He was convinced that "were it not for enemies within the city, there would be no danger from foes without. . . . If it were not for a Brutus, I might live as long as Caesar would have lived."[36] By 1844 the Brutus was known and Joseph's days were numbered.

Notes

1. HC 4:370.

2. HC 3:320.

3. HC 3:423.

4. Smith, *History of Joseph Smith,* p. 301.

5. Ibid., p. 302.

6. Ivan J. Barrett, *Joseph Smith and the Restoration* (Provo, Utah: Young House, 1973), p. 435.

7. Pratt, *Autobiography of Parley P. Pratt,* p. 293.

8. HC 3:375.

9. Smith, *History of Joseph Smith,* p. 304.

10. Matthias F. Cowley, *Wilford Woodruff* (Salt Lake City: Woodruff Family Association, 1909), p. 104.

11. Smith, *History of Joseph Smith,* p. 319.

12. Cowley, *Wilford Woodruff,* p. 105.

13. Smith, *History of Joseph Smith,* pp. 309–10.

14. Ibid., p. 317.

15. HC 5:232.

16. Harvey Cluff Autobiography, typescript, BYU Special Collections, Harold B. Lee Library, Provo, Utah, pp. 4–5.

17. B. H. Roberts, *Comprehensive History of the Church,* 2:161.

18. John L. Butler Autobiography, p. 21, BYU Special Collections, as cited in *LDS Collectors Library* (Salt Lake City: Infobases, 1997).

19. Quoted by Stanley B. Kimball, "Nauvoo," *Improvement Era* 65 (July 1962): 548.

20. E. Cecil McGavin, *Nauvoo, the Beautiful* (Salt Lake City: Stevens & Wallis, 1946), pp. 85–86.

21. Ibid., p. 36.

22. J. Earl Arrington, "William Weeks, Architect of the Nauvoo Temple," *BYU Studies* 19 (Spring 1979): 341.

23. Ibid., p. 346.

24. T. Edgar Lyon, "Recollections of 'Old Nauvooers' Memories from Oral History," *BYU Studies* 18 (Winter 1978): 148.

25. HC 4:492.

26. Wandle Mace Autobiography, p. 94.

27. In JD 5:332.

28. Jane Carter Robinson Hindly, "Jane C. Robinson Hindly Reminiscences and Diary," as cited in Richard Neitzel Holzapfel and Jeni Broberg Holzapfel, *Women of Nauvoo* (Salt Lake City: Bookcraft, 1992), pp. 14–15.

29. HC 6:33.

30. HC 6:165–66.

31. HC 5:166.

32. HC 5:252.

33. Andrus, *They Knew the Prophet,* p. 145.

34. Edwin F. Parry, comp., *Stories about Joseph Smith the Prophet* (Salt Lake City: Deseret News Press, 1934), p. 22.

35. Mercy Thompson, "Recollections," *Juvenile Instructor* 27 (1892): 399.

36. Smith, *History of Joseph Smith,* p. 320.

CHAPTER NINE

THE tentative peace of Nauvoo ended in the winter of 1843–44. Ridicule, arrest warrants, and evil speaking accelerated as Mormon apostates searched for ways to thwart the plans of God and malign the character of his prophet. Doctrines declared sacred by Joseph were distorted to disprove his claims to divine revelation and arouse to new heights angry public sentiment. Unfounded rumors of a secret military invasion of Nauvoo to capture the Mormon prophet were declared as truths.

To Mormons and anti-Mormons alike, an open conflict between the city of Nauvoo and neighbors residing in outlying communities seemed the only alternative to solve the escalating contention. Gun salesmen, believing the conflict inevitable, came to Nauvoo to entice Mormons to buy weapons to defend themselves against imminent danger. Joseph counseled the Saints not to buy weapons: "It would be better to buy ploughshares and raise corn with them. . . . Let us keep cool as a cucumber on a frosty morning."[1]

Keeping calm was not easy for Joseph's followers as enemies with evil intent gathered daily in the nearby community of Carthage. By June 1844 Carthage bulged with malcontents. Yet Joseph remained calm, for he was confident that "all the enemies upon the face of the earth may roar and exert all their power to bring about my death, but they can accomplish nothing, unless some who are among us and enjoy our society . . . join with our enemies." He knew that his "life [was] more in danger from some little dough-head of a fool in this city than from all my numerous and inveterate enemies abroad. I am exposed to far greater danger from traitors among ourselves than from enemies without. . . . *We have a Judas in our midst.*"[2]

Joseph applied the name of Judas to the apostates who had bound themselves together in an oath of conspiracy to seek his life: "You solemnly swear, before God and all holy angels, and these your brethren by whom you are surrounded, that you will give your life, your liberty, your influence, your all, for the destruction of Joseph Smith and his party, so help you God!"[3]

Their avowed malice led the Mormon prophet to muse, "What can be the matter with these men? Is it that the wicked flee when no man pursueth, that hit pigeons always flutter, that drowning men catch at straws, or that [their leaders] Presidents Law and Marks are absolutely traitors to the Church[?]"[4] Although Joseph believed that

I am exposed to far greater danger from traitors among ourselves than from enemies without.

these men "would not scare off an old setting hen," their evil plans ignited public sentiment to a feverish pitch when they printed the *Nauvoo Expositor.*[5] The first and only issue of the newspaper charged Joseph with indulging in whoredoms and abusing political power. It branded him as a base seducer, liar, and murderer. One reader reported that the editors of the *Expositor* "belched forth the most intolerable and the blackest lies that were ever palmed upon a community."[6]

Joseph, acting as mayor of Nauvoo, met with the Nauvoo city council to discuss the libelous accusations printed in the *Expositor.* The official decision stemming from the discussions was to denounce the newspaper as a public nuisance and authorize the Nauvoo sheriff to stop future publication of the *Expositor.* The swift, destructive actions of the sheriff and his posse led publishers of the *Expositor* to charge Joseph and the Nauvoo city council with starting a riot that resulted in the demise of the newspaper.

The incident added fuel to the mounting prejudice and hatred of near neighbors. For example, Thomas Sharp, editor of a small newspaper in Warsaw, Illinois, announced after the *Expositor* incident that "war and extermination is inevitable" against the Mormons of Nauvoo. He encouraged those residing in Warsaw and Carthage to take up arms and destroy the Mormon city: "CITIZENS ARISE, ONE AND ALL!!! Can you stand by, and suffer such INFERNAL DEVILS! to rob men of their property and RIGHTS, without avenging them. We have no time for comment; every man will make his own. LET IT BE MADE WITH POWDER AND BALL!!!"[7]

The inescapable target of the proposed extermination was the prophet-leader Joseph Smith. "Joe Smith, is not safe out of Nauvoo," trumpeted the *Warsaw Signal.* "We would not be surprised to hear of his death by violent means in a short time. He has deadly enemies. . . . The feeling in this county is now lashed to its utmost pitch, and it will break forth in fury upon the slightest provocation."[8]

To Joseph such mobocratic threats were appalling: "I will never tamely submit to the dominion of cursed mobocracy. . . . God Almighty is my shield; and what can man do if God is my friend? I shall not be sacrificed until my time comes; then I shall be offered freely," he said. "I do not regard my own life. I am ready to be offered a sacrifice for this people; for what can our enemies do? Only kill the body, and their power is then at an end."[9]

To his brother Hyrum he cried, "There is no mercy—no mercy here." Hyrum agreed. "Just as sure as we fall into their hands we are dead men." Attempting to escape from the mob element, Joseph and Hyrum left Nauvoo at about two o'clock in the morning of June 23 and were rowed across the Mississippi River to the banks of Iowa. "There is no doubt [the mob element] will come [to Nauvoo] and search for us," Joseph said. "Let them search; they will not harm [the Mormon people]."[10] However, ill-advised friends in Iowa believed the Saints in Nauvoo would be harmed if Joseph and Hyrum did not return. They encouraged the Mormon prophet to face an arraignment in Carthage on the trumped-up charge of riot. With resignation Joseph said, "If my life is of no value to my friends it is of none to myself. . . . *I am going like a lamb to the slaughter, but I am calm as a summer's morning. I have a conscience void of offense toward God and toward all men. If they take my life I shall die an innocent man, and my blood shall cry from the ground for vengeance, and it shall be said of me 'He was murdered in cold blood!'"*[11] He then returned to Nauvoo with his brother Hyrum by his side. They were resigned to their fate: "If we live or have to die, we will be reconciled."[12]

Going as a Lamb

Early Monday morning, June 24, 1844, the Mormon prophet and his brother Hyrum bade farewell to their families in Nauvoo and began their final journey to Carthage. As Joseph gazed upon the city he had orchestrated, he said, "This is the loveliest place and the best people under the heavens; little do they know the trials that await them."[13]

For Joseph and Hyrum, Carthage was a scene of broken promises, illegal arraignment, and incarceration.

Studying the Martyrdom, I thought often of Joseph saying good-bye to his wife and family on that summer morning in Nauvoo. It struck me for the first time that Joseph had left behind a family no different from my own. I thought of the pain Joseph must have felt as he held his wife Emma for the last time. I thought of how his family felt, watching him go. As I continued to think of the farewell, something happened. For the first time in my life, Joseph left the pages of the books and became a living person to me, a man of feelings and sorrows.

Accusations of riot stemming from the *Nauvoo Expositor* incident were turned to treason. Rumors once whispered in secret now were shouted. The militant unabashedly declared that the Smith brothers would not leave Carthage: *"There was nothing against these men; the law could not reach them but powder and ball would,* and they should not go out of Carthage alive."[14]

A mob loitered outside the Carthage jail, where Joseph and Hyrum were imprisoned, and sang, "Where now is the Prophet Joseph? Where now is the Prophet Joseph? Where now is the Prophet Joseph? Safe in Carthage jail!"[15] Even the governor of Illinois, though not a participant in boisterous song, joined the chorus of conspirators, mobbers, and militia in abetting the deaths of Joseph and Hyrum.

A letter written to Emma reveals the sorrowful mood of the Prophet as he contemplated his death: "I am very much resigned to my lot, knowing I am justified, and have done the best that could be done. Give my love to the children and all my friends. . . . May God bless you all."[16]

As the day waned, Joseph and Hyrum and two members of the Quorum of the Twelve Apostles, John Taylor and Willard Richards, lingered in the east bedroom of the Carthage Jail. There Taylor was asked to sing "A Poor Wayfaring Man of Grief." The hymn seemed to harmonize with the ominous foreboding of near events:

> In pris'n I saw him next, condemned
> To meet a traitor's doom at morn.
> The tide of lying tongues I stemmed,
> And honored him 'mid shame and scorn.
> My friendship's utmost zeal to try,
> He asked if I for him would die.
> The flesh was weak; my blood ran chill,
> But my free spirit cried, "I will!"[17]

Around five in the afternoon of June 27, 1844, Richards saw a hundred or more men running around the corner of the jail. Taylor described them as "an armed mob—painted black—of from 150 to 200 persons."[18]

Joseph knew of his impending death. I believe
Hyrum did too. The brothers had been
together most of their lives. Hyrum
had been at Joseph's side to
encourage, advise, and protect.
Now imprisoned, Hyrum,
who would not leave Joseph to
suffer a martyr's fate alone,
would also seal his testimony
with his blood.

They easily overpowered the jailor, rushed the stairs, and began shooting into the east bedroom. Despite initial attempts to protect themselves from mob violence, the four men were no match for the disguised mobbers.

Hyrum was the first to fall from an assassin's bullet. As he backed away from the door to the center of the thigh. A bullet from the outside hit the watch in his vest. After he crawled under a bed for protection, he was hit by three additional bullets: one below the left knee, another in his hip, and a third in the fore-part of his left arm. His life spared, Taylor would one day become President of the Church.

This is my favorite painting in the show. It is the first painting I did of the Prophet Joseph Smith. When I started working on it, I thought I knew who Joseph Smith was. Looking back, I realize I knew things about him, but I did not know him. Over the past couple of years I have come to understand a little better who the Prophet Joseph Smith really is. ✍ I started seeing the human side of Joseph when I understood that he cared more for his brother's life than for his own. When Joseph decided to return to Carthage and stand trial, Hyrum insisted on coming with him. Joseph begged Hyrum to stay behind, but Hyrum refused. Joseph must have known he was going to die; I am sure he wanted to spare Hyrum's life. But Hyrum was Joseph's companion in death just as he had always been in life. ✍ What a price was paid for each of us. May we never forget.

room, one bullet pierced the upper panel of the door and struck him on the left side of the nose. As he was falling to the floor, he exclaimed, "*I am a dead man!*"[19] Bending over the body of his lifeless brother, Joseph sobbed, "Oh dear, brother Hyrum!"[20] Hyrum was hit by three other bullets—one entered his left side, another his head near his throat, and the third lodged in his left leg.

Taylor was the second to be shot by the murderous mob. As he attempted to leap out the east window of the bedroom, a bullet fired from the doorway struck his

Willard Richards, the fourth prisoner, lived in fulfillment of Joseph's earlier prophecy that Willard would "stand where the balls will fly around you like hail and men will fall dead by your side, and . . . there never shall a ball injure you."[21]

As Joseph moved toward the east bedroom window, two bullets hit him from the doorway, and two struck him from the outside. He fell from the second-story window to the ground below and was heard to exclaim, "*O Lord my God!*"[22] The mob had finished its murderous plot

Oh, My Poor Dear Brother Hyrum

and Joseph, the Prophet, lay dead outside of the jail.

A tearful message announcing the martyrdom of the Smith brothers was sent to Nauvoo: "Joseph and Hyrum are dead. . . . The job was done in an instant."[23] Illinois governor Thomas Ford, believing the Mormons of Nauvoo would pillage and destroy Carthage upon learning of the death of Joseph, "advised all who were present [in Carthage] to disperse, as he expected the Mormons would be so exasperated that they would come and burn the town."[24] Retaliation was not the issue for most Latter-day Saints, although Allen Stout's journal entry may typify the anguish of some: "I knew not how to contain myself. . . . I feel like cutting their throats."[25] The issue for the gentler Saint was lamentation and preparation for the return of the cortege to Nauvoo.

About 8:00 A.M. on Friday, June 28, the remains of Joseph and Hyrum were placed in rough boxes, put into two wagons, and then covered with prairie hay, blankets, and bushes to protect them from the hot sun. A guard of eight soldiers led by Samuel Smith was detached to escort the remains to Nauvoo. Between 2:30 and 3:00 P.M. the procession moved slowly along Mulholland Street in Nauvoo, where the assembled Nauvoo Legion, the city council, and thousands of mourners vented their sorrow.

"Such mourning and lamentation was seldom ever heard on the earth," wrote Sarah Leavitt.[26] Dan Jones descriptively penned, "Oh, the sorrowful scene to be seen in Nauvoo that day! There has never been nor will there ever be anything like it; everyone sad along the streets, all the shops closed and every business forgotten."[27] The procession proceeded down Main Street to the Mansion House, where the bodies were taken into the dining room and the door closed. "As they drove around to the Mansion," Mary Rich penned, "the people were almost frantic to get one little glimpse of him, but they were driven back by the marshall. The wagon was driven inside of the back gate and the gate was locked. No one was allowed in the yard except the guards and the Prophet's special friends."[28]

The eight to ten thousand Saints assembled near the Mansion House heard brief remarks from Church leaders. Most remembered were the words of Willard Richards, who "had pledged his honor, and his life for their good conduct." The people "with one united voice resolved to trust to the law for a remedy of such a high-handed assassination, and when that failed, to call upon God to avenge them of their wrongs."[29] Those assembled were admonished to go quietly home and promised that beginning at eight o'clock the next morning, June 29, the remains of the martyrs could be viewed by all.

In the meanwhile, inside the Mansion House the bodies were washed in preparation for the private and public viewing. Camphor-soaked cotton was placed in each gunshot wound and the bodies dressed in "fine plain drawers and shirt, white neckerchiefs, white cotton stockings and white shrouds."[30] Afterward the bodies were first viewed by remaining family members. "I had for a long time braced every nerve, roused every energy of my soul and called upon God to strengthen me," said Mother Smith, "but when I entered the room and saw my murdered sons extended both at once before my eyes and heard the sobs and groans of my family and the cries of

'Father! Husband! Brothers!' from the lips of their wives, children, brothers and sisters, it was too much; I sank back, crying to the Lord in the agony of my soul, 'My God, my God, why hast thou forsaken this family!'" In reply Mother Smith heard a voice say to her, "I have taken them to myself, that they might have rest."[31]

At 7:00 A.M. on Saturday, June 29, the bodies were placed in white cambric-lined coffins that were covered with black velvet and fastened with brass nails. Over the face of each corpse was a lid, hung with brass hinges, that held a square of glass. At 8:00 A.M. the public viewing began. "Thousands came from all quarters to take a last look; and steamboats loaded with strangers came from Burlington, Quincy and many other places, to look upon their dead bodies," reported Sarah Rich.[32] It was estimated that "over ten thousand persons visited the remains" from 8:00 A.M. to 5:00 P.M., entering at the west door and exiting at the north door of the Mansion House.[33]

"The [martyrs'] heads were placed to the north. As we came in at the door," penned Mosiah Hancock, "we came to the feet of the Prophet Joseph, then passed up by his left side and around his head, then down by his right side. Next we turned to the right and came to the feet of Hyrum, then up by his left side and around his head and down by his right side, then we filed out of the other door."[34] Dan Jones wrote, "Each in his turn the thousands made their way forward, sad and desirous of having the last look at their dear brethren whose solemn counsels and heavenly teaching had been music in their ears, lighting their paths and bringing joy to their hearts on numerous occasions."[35] At five o'clock in the afternoon the Mansion House was cleared of the mourners and the family was invited to make their final farewells. The coffins were then concealed in a bedroom closet in the northeast corner of the home. Carefully placed into the awaiting hearse were rough pine boxes filled with bags of sand instead of the martyrs' remains. When the funeral procession began, the cortege moved down Main Street, passed by the temple,

Each in his turn the thousands made their way forward, sad and desirous of having the last look at their dear brethren.

and stopped at the burial vault. A burial was staged.

At about midnight on June 29, long after the mourners had retired, the coffins containing the bodies were taken from the Mansion House and carried through the garden, around the pump, and to the Nauvoo House. The bodies were interred in the basement story of the uncompleted structure. After the burial the ground was flattened and covered with chips of wood, stone, and other rubbish to camouflage the site. That night a violent rainstorm removed any trace of the actual site of the burial.

Although the martyrs' burial site was obscured, the accomplishments of the life of the Prophet Joseph Smith will never be blurred. The testimony of Joseph lives on. Through eternity he will be numbered with the sanctified and the religious martyrs of all ages. "It is by no means improbable that some future textbook," said Josiah

Quincy, a former mayor of Boston, "will contain a question something like this: What historical American of the nineteenth century has exerted the most powerful influence upon the destinies of his countrymen? And it is by no means impossible that the answer to that interrogatory may be thus written: Joseph Smith, the Mormon Prophet."[36]

To this we also testify—Joseph was a modern prophet of the Lord. And together with John Taylor we proclaim, "Joseph Smith, the Prophet and Seer of the Lord, has done more, save Jesus only, for the salvation of men in this world, than any other man that ever lived in it. . . . [He has] left a fame and name that cannot be slain. He lived great, and he died great in the eyes of God and his people; and like most of the Lord's anointed in ancient times, has sealed his mission and his works with his own blood."[37]

Notes

1. *HC* 6:151–52.

2. *HC* 6:152.

3. Horace Cummings, "Conspiracy of Nauvoo," *Contributor* 5 (April 1884): 255.

4. *HC* 6:170.

5. *HC* 6:272.

6. Smith, *History of Joseph Smith,* p. 322.

7. *Warsaw Signal,* 12 June 1844, as cited in Roger D. Launius, "Anti-Mormonism in Illinois: Thomas C. Sharp's Unfinished History of the Mormon War, 1845," *Journal of Mormon History* 15 (1989): 30.

8. *Warsaw Signal,* 29 May 1844.

9. *HC* 6:499; 5:259; 6:500.

10. *HC* 6:545.

11. *HC* 6:549, 555.

12. *HC* 6:550.

13. *HC* 6:554.

14. *HC* 6:566.

15. Roberts, *Comprehensive History,* 2:281.

16. *HC* 6:605.

17. *Hymns of The Church of Jesus Christ of Latter-day Saints* (Salt Lake City: The Church of Jesus Christ of Latter-day Saints, 1985), no. 29.

18. D&C 135:1.

19. D&C 135:1.

20. *HC* 6:618.

21. Recollection of Brigham Young, unpublished discourse of 14 July 1861, LDS Church Archives; as cited in Truman G. Madsen, *Joseph Smith the Prophet* (Salt Lake City: Bookcraft, 1989), pp. 123–24.

22. D&C 135:1.

23. *HC* 6:621–22.

24. *HC* 6:625.

25. Journal of Allen Joseph Stout, typescript, BYU Special Collections, p. 19.

26. Sarah Leavitt History, 1919, p. 22, as cited in *LDS Collectors Library* (Salt Lake City: Infobases, 1997).

27. "I shall ever remember my feelings," *Church News,* 24 June 1984, 11 (translated from the original Welsh by Ronald D. Dennis).

28. Mary Rich Autobiography, typescript,

BYU Special Collections, p. 17.

29. *HC* 6:626.

30. *HC* 6:627.

31. Smith, *History of Joseph Smith,* p. 324.

32. Sarah Rich Autobiography, typescript, BYU Special Collections, p. 40.

33. *HC* 6:627.

34. Mosiah Hancock Autobiography, typescript, BYU Special Collections, pp. 29–30.

35. *Church News,* 24 June 1984.

36. Roberts, *Comprehensive History,* 2:349–50.

37. D&C 135:3.

My Servant Joseph

Bibliography

Andrus, Hyrum L., and Helen Mae Andrus, comps. *They Knew the Prophet.* Salt Lake City: Bookcraft, 1974.

Arrington, J. Earl. "William Weeks, Architect of the Nauvoo Temple." *BYU Studies* 19 (Spring 1979): 341.

Backman, Milton V., Jr. *The Heavens Resound: A History of the Latter-day Saints in Ohio 1830–1838.* Salt Lake City: Deseret Book, 1983.

———. *Joseph Smith's First Vision.* Salt Lake City: Bookcraft, 1971.

Barrett, Ivan J. *Joseph Smith and the Restoration.* Provo, Utah: Brigham Young University Press, 1967.

———. *Young Joseph.* N.p.: RIC Publishing, 1981.

Brown, Benjamin. *Testimonies for the Truth.* Liverpool: S. W. Richards, 1853.

Bushman, Richard L. *Joseph Smith and the Beginnings of Mormonism.* Chicago: University of Illinois Press, 1984.

Butler, John L. Autobiography. Special Collections. Brigham Young University Library. As cited in *LDS Collectors Library* [CD-ROM]. Provo, Utah: Infobases International, 1997.

Cannon, Donald Q., and Lyndon W. Cook, eds. *Far West Record: Minutes of The Church of Jesus Christ of Latter-day Saints, 1830–1844.* Salt Lake City: Deseret Book, 1983.

Clark, John B., to Lilburn W. Boggs. As cited in Leland Gentry. "A History of the Latter-day Saints in Northern Missouri from 1836 to 1839." Ph.D. dissertation, Brigham Young University, 1965, p. 544.

Cluff, Harvey. Autobiography. Typescript. Special Collections. Brigham Young University Library.

Cope, Kenneth. *My Servant Joseph* [CD album]. Midvale, Utah: Embryo Music, 1993.

Cowley, Matthias F. *Wilford Woodruff.* Salt Lake City: Woodruff Family Association, 1909.

Cummings, Horace. "Conspiracy of Nauvoo." *Contributor* 5 (April 1884): 255.

Dennis, Ronald D., trans. "I shall ever remember my feelings." *Church News,* 24 June 1984, p. 11.

"Experiences in the Life of Rhoda Ann Fullmer." Copy in author's possession.

Garrard, LaMar E.. "The Asael Smith Family Moves from Vermont to New York, 1806–1820." In *Regional Studies in Latter-day Saint Church History: New York.* Ed. Larry C. Porter, Milton V. Backman, Jr., and Susan Easton Black. Provo, Utah: Brigham Young University, Department of Church History and Doctrine, 1992.

Geauga Gazette, 17 April 1832. As cited in Max H. Parkin. *Conflict at Kirtland: A Study of the Nature and Causes of External and Internal Conflicts of the Mormons in Ohio between 1830 and 1838.* Salt Lake City: Max Parkin, 1967.

Hale, Isaac. Statement. As reprinted in Emily C. Blackman. *History of Susquehanna County, Pennsylvania.* Philadelphia: Claxton, Remsen, and Haffelfinger, 1873.

Hancock, Levi Ward. Autobiography. Typescript. Special Collections. Brigham Young University Library.

Hancock, Mosiah. Autobiography. Typescript. Special Collections. Brigham Young University Library.

Hindly, Jane Carter Robinson. "Jane Robinson Hindly Reminiscences and Diary." As cited in Richard Neitzel Holzapfel and Jeni Broberg Holzapfel. *Women of Nauvoo.* Salt Lake City: Bookcraft, 1992.

Howe, Eber D. *Mormonism Unvailed.* Painesville, Ohio: E. D. Howe, 1834.

Huntington Library Letters, microfilm no. 87. As cited in Stanley R. Gunn. *Oliver Cowdery, Second Elder and Scribe.* Salt Lake City: Bookcraft, 1962.

Huntington, William. Journal. Copy in author's possession.

Hymns of The Church of Jesus Christ of Latter-day Saints. Salt Lake City:

The Church of Jesus Christ of Latter-day Saints, 1985.

Jenson, Andrew. *Latter-day Saints' Biographical Encyclopedia.* 4 vols. Salt Lake City: Deseret News, 1901–36.

Johnson, Benjamin. "My Life's Review." As cited in Backman, *The Heavens Resound,* p. 143.

Johnson, Clark V., ed. *Mormon Redress Petitions: Documents of the 1833–1838 Missouri Conflict.* Provo, Utah: Brigham Young University, Religious Studies Center, 1992.

Journal of Discourses. Reported by G. D. Watt. 26 vols. 1854–86. Reprint, Salt Lake City: Lithographic Reprints, 1966.

Kennedy, Inez A. *Recollections of the Pioneers of Lee County.* Dixon, Ill.: n.p., 1893. As cited in Linda King Newell and Valeen Tippetts Avery. *Mormon Enigma: Emma Hale Smith.* New York: Doubleday, 1984.

Kimball, Stanley B. "Nauvoo." *Improvement Era* 65 (July 1962): 548.

Knight, Newel. "Newel Knight's Journal." In *Classic Experiences and Adventures.* Salt Lake City: Bookcraft, 1969.

"Last Testimony of Sister Emma." *Saints' Herald* 26 (1 October 1879): 289–90. As cited in Milton V. Backman, Jr. *Eyewitness Accounts of the Restoration.* Orem, Utah: Grandin Book, 1983. P. 54.

Latter-day Saints' Messenger and Advocate, December 1834, p. 40.

Leavitt, Sarah. History. As cited in *LDS Collectors Library* [CD-ROM]. Provo, Utah: Infobases, 1997.

"Letter from Elder W. H. Kelley." *Saints' Herald,* 1 March 1882, p. 68.

Lightner, Mary E. Address delivered at Brigham Young University, Provo, Utah, 14 April 1905. Copy in Archives. Brigham Young University Library.

Lyon, T. Edgar. "Recollections of 'Old Nauvooers' Memories from Oral History." *BYU Studies* 18 (Winter 1978): 148.

Mace, Wandle. Autobiography. Typescript. Special Collections. Brigham Young University Library.

McGavin, E. Cecil. *Nauvoo, the Beautiful.* Salt Lake City: Stevens & Wallis, 1946.

Minutes of the Salt Lake City School of the Prophets, 10–11 October 1883. As cited in Andrus, *They Knew the Prophet.*

Moffit, John Clifton. "Isaac Morley on the American Frontier." Copy in author's possession.

Nibley, Preston. *Witnesses of the Book of Mormon.* Salt Lake City: Stevens and Wallis, 1946.

Parry, Edwin F., comp. *Stories about Joseph Smith the Prophet.* Salt Lake City: Deseret News Press, 1934.

Peterson, J. W. "William Smith Interview." *Deseret Evening News,* 28 (20 January 1894): 11.

Porter, Larry C. "A Study of the Origins of The Church of Jesus Christ of Latter-day Saints in the States of New York and Pennsylvania, 1816–1831." Ph.D. dissertation, Brigham Young University, 1971.

Pratt, Orson. *An Interesting Account of Several Remarkable Visions.* Edinburgh: Ballantyne & Hughes, 1840.

Pratt, Parley P. *Autobiography of Parley P. Pratt.* Salt Lake City: Deseret Book, 1980.

Rich, Mary. Autobiography. Typescript. Special Collections. Brigham Young University Library.

Rich, Sarah. Autobiography. Typescript. Special Collections. Brigham Young University Library.

Roberts, B. H. *A Comprehensive History of The Church of Jesus Christ of Latter-day Saints.* 6 vols. Provo, Utah: Brigham Young University Press, 1965.

Robinson, E. "Items of Person History." *The Return,* 2 (March 1890): 16, 234. As cited in Stephen C. LeSueur. *The 1838 Mormon War in Missouri.* Columbia, Missouri: University of Missouri Press, 1987.

Salisbury, Katherine. "Dear Sisters." *Saints' Herald* 33 (1 May 1886): 260.

Scraps of Biography, Faith-Promoting Series. Salt Lake City: Juvenile Instructor Office, 1883.

"Sketch of the Auto-biography of George Albert Smith." *Millennial Star* 27 (15 July 1865): 439.

Smith, Emma. Interview of Emma Smith Bidamon by Nels Madson and Parley P. Pratt, Jr., 1877. Archives Division, Church Historical Department, The Church of Jesus Christ of Latter-day Saints, Salt Lake City, Utah.

Smith, George A. Journal, 25 June 1834. George A. Smith Family Papers. Special Collections. Marriott Library, University of Utah.

Smith, Hedde M. P. "The Life of Thomas Grover, Utah Pioneer." Closure project, Brigham Young University Independent Study. Collections–Storage. Brigham Young University Library.

Smith, John A. Journal, 23 April 1838. George A. Smith Family Papers. Special Collections. Marriott Library, University of Utah.

Smith, Joseph. Affidavit of Joseph Smith et al., 15 March 1839. As cited in Heman C. Smith, ed. "Appeals to Supreme Court of Missouri." *Journal of History* 9 (April 1916): 206.

———. "Manuscript History of the Church," Book A-1. As quoted in Reed C. Durham, Jr. "Joseph Smith's Own Story of Serious Childhood Illness." *BYU Studies* 10 (Summer 1970): 481.

———. To Emma Smith, 12 November 1838. As cited in Smith, *Personal Writings of Joseph Smith.*

———. *History of The Church of Jesus Christ of Latter-day Saints.* Ed. Brigham H. Roberts. 7 vols. Salt Lake City: Deseret Book, 1932.

———. *The Personal Writings of Joseph Smith.* Comp. Dean C. Jessee. Salt Lake City: Deseret Book, 1984.

Smith, Joseph Fielding. *Essentials of Church History.* Salt Lake City: Deseret Book, 1953.

Smith, Lucy Mack. *Biographical Sketches of Joseph Smith, the Prophet, and His Progenitors for Many Generations.* London and Liverpool: S. W. Richards, 1853. Reprint ed., New York: Arno Press and the New York Times, 1969.

———. *History of Joseph Smith by His Mother.* Ed. Preston Nibley. Salt Lake City: Bookcraft, 1956.

———. "Manuscript History of Her Son Joseph Smith, Jr." As quoted in Donald L. Enders. "The Joseph Smith, Sr., Family: Farmers of the Genessee." In *Joseph Smith: The Prophet, The Man.* Ed. Susan Easton Black and Charles D. Tate, Jr. Provo, Utah: Brigham Young University, Religious Studies Center, 1993.

———. "Preliminary Manuscript of Biographical Sketches of Joseph Smith." Typescript. Archives Division, Church Historical Department, The Church of Jesus Christ of Latter-day Saints, Salt Lake City, Utah.

Stout, Allen Joseph. Journal. Typescript. Special Collections. Brigham Young University Library.

The Juvenile Instructor 17 (1 October 1882): 302.

Thompson, Mercy. "Recollections." *Juvenile Instructor* 27 (1892): 399.

Tucker, Pomeroy. *Origin, Rise, and Progress of Mormonism: Biography of its founders and history of its church: personal remembrances and historical collections hitherto unwritten.* New York: D. Appleton and Co., 1867.

Tullidge, Edward W. *The Women of Mormondom.* New York: n.p., 1877.

Warsaw Signal, 12 June 1844, as cited in Roger D. Launius. "Anti-Mormonism in Illinois: Thomas C. Sharp's Unfinished History of the Mormon War, 1845." *Journal of Mormon History* 15 (1989): 30.

Watson, Elden Jay. *Manuscript History of Brigham Young, 1801–1844.* Salt Lake City: n.p., 1968.

Whitmer, David. *An Address to All Believers in Christ.* Richmond, Missouri: n.p., 1887.

Whitney, Orson F. *Life of Heber C. Kimball, an Apostle; the Father and Founder of the British Mission.* Salt Lake City: Juvenile Instructor Office, 1888.

Woodruff, Wilford. Journal History. As quoted in Preston Nibley, *Presidents of the Church.* Salt Lake City: Deseret Book, 1941.

Young, Brigham. Recollection of Brigham Young, unpublished discourse of 14 July 1861. Typescript. LDS Church Archives. As cited in Truman G. Madsen, *Joseph Smith the Prophet.* Salt Lake City: Bookcraft, 1989.